Tails from the Reedbed

Tails from the Reedbed

A study of **otters** at
Leighton Moss

ELAINE PRINCE

First published in 2019
by Palatine Books, Carnegie House, Chatsworth Road,
Lancaster LA1 4SL
www.carnegiepublishing.com

British Library Cataloguing-in-Publication data
A catalogue record for this book is available from the
British Library

Paperback ISBN 13: 978-1-910837-20-7

Designed and typeset by Carnegie Book Production

Printed and bound by Cambrian Printers

Foreword

For any ornithologist, Leighton Moss is a paradise, known throughout the country. Not just to ornithologists, of course, but for any naturalist it has an unparalleled richness of wildlife, of water, reedbeds and natural open spaces, with lots of places where one can easily watch all this without causing disturbance. It is one of the best places in England to see that elusive symbol of elegant beauty, the otter.

Elaine Prince has used this unique opportunity offered by Leighton Moss more than anyone else, and here she describes her breathtaking encounters with the animals in lovely detail. She shows how much a visitor can see of the behaviour of the otters by just watching from one of the several marvellous bird-hides on the reserve, and writes about this with such wonderful directness that one sits in the hide with her, taking in the antics of the otters' cubs, the mating of a particular male otter called 'Kinky', a mother looking after the young ones, otters catching eels right in front of one.

There is something magical about otters, something that makes the animal as popular as it is despite very few people ever seeing it. Even when lucky enough to watch one, rarely do we see the whole animal, usually only the top of a head, a tail, with a stir along the surface. Yet the behaviour is all there and one never tires of the excitement of an otter watch, seeing grace through the ripples, with always something new.

This little book brings this home through the eyes of an experienced observer, of someone with ultimate patience and who can write about it. It will make one wish to be there in the hide, to experience the wonderful scenery of Leighton Moss with not only otters, but also a bittern, some egrets, a marsh harrier that upsets the ducks. Against all this rich tapestry of birds, it is great to find how much one can learn from these pages about the otters' behaviour, their mating, looking after cubs, catching eels. A beautiful piece of work!

Hans Kruuk

Introduction

Leighton Moss RSPB held a healthy population of otters up until the early 1990s, when they suffered a sudden and dramatic decline, and this is discussed in an appendix to this book, beginning at page 109.

John Wilson, the founding warden of Leighton Moss, logged his final otter record in 1997, and there followed a number of years with no further evidence.

Then, around 2006, there were intermittent reports of spraint on the causeway and under the railway bridge at the wader pools, but no confirmed sightings. Otters were returning, or had returned, to former haunts all over the country, and Leighton Moss was clearly being investigated, so it seemed only a matter of time before they put in a more visible appearance.

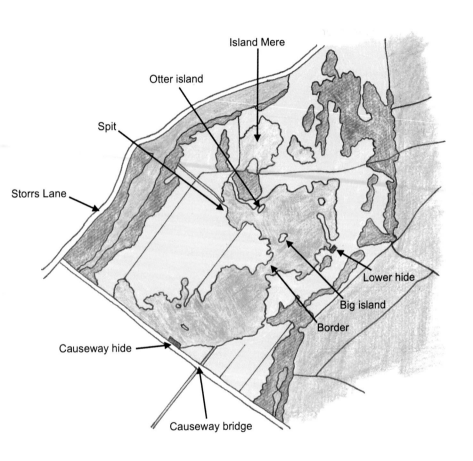

Island Mere

Otter island

Spit

Storrs Lane

Lower hide

Big island

Border

Causeway hide

Causeway bridge

This book contains some of my observations over the years 2006 to 2016, transcribed from the field notes I made at the time, mostly at dusk and dawn. I have included only those events that were especially memorable for one reason or another, along with those that best demonstrated the changes I saw in otter populations at Leighton Moss over the course of that decade.

Whilst watching otters, or often whilst waiting for them, I enjoyed many other wildlife encounters, and I have also described some of these in my account.

In order to better define my records I named a number of landmarks, and these are shown on the map opposite, which is a plan view of the reserve to the north east of the causeway. This is the area where otters were most often seen, and is therefore where my efforts were concentrated. The map is drawn to scale, and gives some indication of the spatial relationships between the landmarks that I used.

The parallel lines in the reedbed depict the main drainage channels, though there are also others that I have not included. By means of these channels otters can travel across much of the reserve without showing themselves at all, which explains some of the remarkable disappearing acts for which they are renowned.

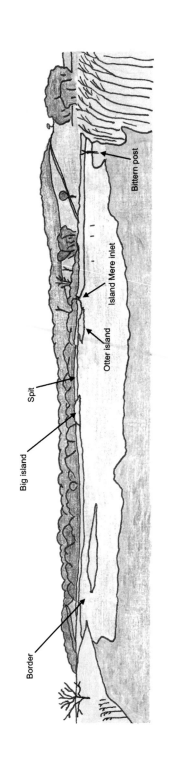

Border

Big island

Spit

Otter island

Island Mere inlet

Bittern post

The sketch on the facing page shows these same features to scale as seen from Lower hide;

There are three posts to the right of Island Mere inlet that I also used as landmarks (or watermarks?). These have always been favourite perches for cormorants, which often sit there to dry their wings, and they are also useful aids for determining water levels. The left post is the shortest, so is the first to disappear from view as levels rise, and when all three are underwater then it's time to dust off my wellingtons.

Lower and Causeway hides both lie on the shore of the same body of water, but I refer to the areas in front of them as Lower and Causeway pools. Between the two pools there is a constriction, which I refer to as the Border.

Lower pool extends some distance in front of the hide, and behind Big and Otter islands there is a small bay, where the Spit is located, a popular nesting area for many species of birds.

Lower hide itself was built in 1990 by RSPB wardens John Wilson and David Mower, with the assistance of a young volunteer called Jarrod Sneyd, who nowadays is the site manager at Leighton Moss. Jarrod recalls that they were watched by two otters, which approached quite closely and seemed undeterred by the noise of the construction.

Island Mere is a substantial body of water, which can be viewed from the road, but which is not visible from Lower hide. Island Mere inlet is an access point that otters often use to pass between Lower pool and Island Mere.

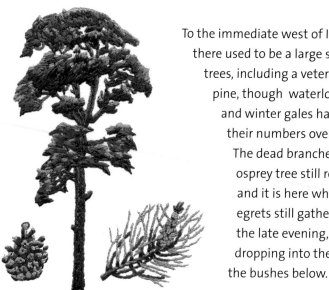

To the immediate west of Island Mere there used to be a large stand of trees, including a veteran Scots pine, though waterlogged roots and winter gales have thinned their numbers over the years. The dead branches of the osprey tree still remain, and it is here where the egrets still gather in the late evening, before dropping into their roost in the bushes below.

The Bittern post is so named because it was one of the favourite haunts of a female bittern which had been ringed on the reserve as a chick in 2000, and whose ring I managed to read for the first time in 2005. Reading and photographing this ring subsequently became a popular sport at Leighton Moss for a number of years. To the best of my knowledge a photograph taken on 26th April 2012 was the last record of this bird, and confirmed its status as the UK's oldest known bittern at that time.

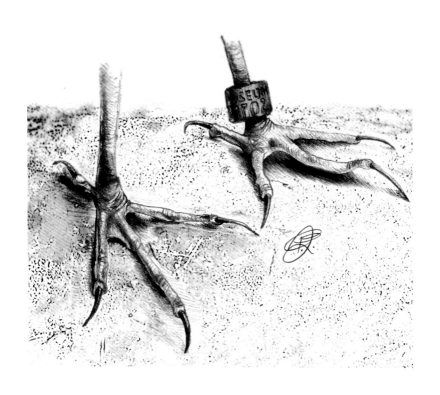

Chapter One

My first sighting was on the 8th March 2006, on a wet misty morning in Lower hide. Visibility was so poor that I could only just make out the three posts in front of the window, and nothing much seemed to be happening.

Then, in a heart stopping moment, an otter loomed out of the mist in front of the posts, grappling with an eel. It headed straight towards the hide, causing me severe palpitations as I struggled to assemble my scope, which was completely unnecessary since the animal was so close I hardly needed binoculars! Suddenly, as fast as it had appeared, it dived and was gone.

I had been a regular visitor to Leighton Moss for many years but had never seen an otter before, yet this was infinitely more moving than I could possibly have anticipated, despite its brevity. I had absolutely no idea at that time, however, just how familiar these animals were going to become over the forthcoming years.

A week later, in the early hours of the morning, Robin Horner, the site manager at that time, was monitoring elvers at the tidal sluice between the Allen/Morecambe pools and the reserve. This was part of the RSPB's long-term study of the eel population, but led to an unexpected and very close brush with an otter. The animal attempted to pass through the tidal flap onto the saltmarsh, but on seeing Robin it flipped over and headed back towards Leighton Moss. This was to be one of the very few times they were ever actually seen away from the reedbed, even though I often found spraint under the railway bridge.

Our initial excitement at the apparent return of otters to Leighton Moss proved to be somewhat premature, as there were no further reports for over nine months, so possibly we had been visited by a lone individual which had since moved on.

Then, in late December 2006, two otters were seen at Lower hide, so it looked as though they might be back. I therefore began my dawn and dusk vigils, which were to occupy me for the next ten years.

My efforts were rewarded at the beginning of a bitterly cold January day in 2007, when two otters crossed swiftly from Otter island to Big island. They cavorted for some time, facing each other off with open mouths, then porpoised rapidly and purposefully back to Otter island, where they went back into the reeds.

At the end of the month, in freezing conditions, two otters traversed the ice going towards Island Mere, and with them out of the water I could see that one was larger than the other.

I saw only one or two otters over the next two months, but being on the reserve at the most exciting parts of the day inevitably resulted in other wildlife events, such as the one I shared on a memorable Sunday evening at the end of March.

The evening began with black-headed gulls diving on an area of reedbed, where there was a bittern half-hidden in the reeds. The bittern took off, and flew right across the water from left to right, illuminated by the setting sun and escorted by the gulls. Two great crested grebes began their weed dance display, a performance I never tire of watching.

Three lads from Liverpool, Danny, Paul and Mick, arrived, bristling with video technology and eager to record footage of the much publicised otters. I warned them that there had been no sightings for a couple of weeks, so they couldn't be counted on, but I felt sure that something was bound to turn up to make their visit worthwhile.

Almost immediately, 23 whooper swans flew in from the west and landed on the water, honking noisily. Taking exception to this intrusion, the two resident mute swans charged the whoopers in full threat posture. Swimming in from either side they managed to split the group into two, but the whoopers stood their ground in increasingly vociferous agitation. Not content with this the male mute swan launched itself at the main group, violently attacking several of its members.

All of the whoopers took to the air, circled around a couple of times, and then, obviously choosing discretion over valour, retreated in the direction from which they had arrived.

A flock of starlings performed their aerial magic in front of the hide, followed by sand martins, flying low over the water at first, before grouping up high above. A noisy bunch of pied wagtails gathered on the sparse reeds in front of the window, the slender stems barely supporting their weight. One by one they melted into the reedbed, and their chattering gradually subsided, leaving an atmospheric silence, as darkness fell.

We peered hopefully into the night, though we felt sure we had almost certainly already seen the final act, and were ready to call it a day.

I put the cap on my scope, and reached forward to close the window, but out of the corner of my eye I glimpsed a movement in the water. I quietly alerted the others, and we all watched as an otter made its way along the length of the hide, only a stone's throw away, before finally heading off towards the Border. The lads from Liverpool were over the moon, as they had managed to record the whole performance on video, which probably still lurks somewhere on YouTube to this day.

The sunset wasn't bad either ...

Through the spring, and into summer, there were intermittent reports of one or two otters from various parts of the reserve.

Towards the end of May water levels were much higher than usual. A spectacular midge eruption filled the air with clouds of insects, so small and so numerous that they gave the appearance of columns of smoke spiralling from the water. The fish rising to take advantage of this bounty produced countless overlapping ripples, rendering otter spotting somewhat challenging. Nevertheless, I eventually managed to find a single otter, which appeared from the right of Lower hide. It then headed towards Island Mere, where it flushed a bittern, which was immediately mobbed by a marsh harrier, and for a moment I had all three in a single view through my scope, making this something of a red-letter moment.

On another occasion the presence of an otter was revealed by the antics of a huge raft of flightless coots and ducks, all trying to put as much distance as possible between it and them. The collective sound of their fluttering across the pool sounded like a waterfall, and, in the gap they had created, an otter surfaced. I've seen flightless birds spooked by cormorants, great-crested grebes, marsh harriers and pike, but nothing moves them quite like an otter!

As summer wore on I began to notice a regular pattern of behaviour from a single otter that appeared from behind Big island in the late evening. It swam fast and purposefully, crossing the pool from left to right as though it was on a mission, always entering the reeds at exactly the same spot.

By the beginning of September the behaviour of this particular otter had become very predictable indeed, though views were often so short and fast that you could easily have blinked and missed them.

Interestingly, I had started to time my observations, which always seemed longer than they really were, and I estimated that in a whole week I probably watched an otter for a total of only about two and a half minutes.

Around the middle of the month, the otter, which I now thought to be a female, was swimming its usual course. I noted that whereas it usually navigated this route at high speed, this time it was travelling much more slowly. Then, just as it went into the reeds, I fancied I saw a disturbance in the water behind it, and in the failing light I had a tantalisingly brief glimpse of what appeared to be two very small heads.

'Looks like we have cubs,' I thought, almost disbelievingly.

Although there was no real alternative explanation of what I had just seen, I wanted better views in order to be absolutely sure.

After all, these were the first cubs on the reserve for many years, and something of a milestone. I therefore watched well into the darkness every night, but confirmation was to take quite a while longer than I expected.

The following evening brought a strong wind with heavy rain causing turbulent conditions, with hardly any wildfowl to alert me to otter movement. The little egrets had all dropped down into their roost next to Island Mere. A small flock of pintails flew in and splashed about near Big island, then moved over to the Spit to join the mallards.

I was scanning the reed edge, and in the twilight I just managed to see an otter, heading right. It passed behind the island and continued on towards the Inlet, swimming very slowly. It often paused and turned to look back, but, despite careful searching, it was too dark for me to see anything else in the choppy water.

I continued my nightly observations but saw nothing more until early October, when I picked out a wake moving right from Big island, an otter moving very quickly and breaking the surface only occasionally. It was an adult, followed closely by a second smaller individual.

It had taken me twenty days, but I could at last confirm that this was indeed a cub, which was swimming confidently, and was now easy to see in the calm water. The two otters crossed the pool and entered the reeds at the far right, but there was no sign of the second cub. I scanned the route they had taken and after what seemed an age, but was probably no more than a minute, I spotted a second small otter. It followed exactly the same route, propelling itself along with short rapid dives, and disappeared at the same point.

As autumn progressed I saw the cubs growing in both size and confidence, often swimming in close formation, coiling around each other or play fighting.

On one occasion, in the dimming light, they lingered close to the hide, and for the first time I could hear them squeaking and whistling to each other. The female was nowhere to be seen, and had left the cubs to fend for themselves whilst she went off to fish alone, which is quite normal behaviour. A female otter will also often leave her cubs on dry land while she hunts, and there are many accounts from other sites of otter cubs being 'rescued' by well-meaning members of the public, who have wrongly assumed that they had been abandoned.

December began. The weather became increasingly wet, and water levels started to rise. Temperatures fell, and the edges of the pools froze, but I still saw otters regularly.

I noted, however, that finding of spraint did not seem to be reliable as an indication of the presence of otters, as there was often a lack of spraint in the usual areas even when I had good sightings. Of course they could have been spraining on routes to which I had no access, but conversely I also often saw spraint in the usual areas when I had no sight of the animals themselves.

The rain continued into the New Year of 2008, and by mid-January the water on Lower hide path was nearly over the top of my wellingtons. When I reached the hide I found spraint on the steps, and as I opened the window an otter was so close that I could almost have reached out and touched it.

The paths remained flooded until February, and I wondered whether I should buy a rubber dinghy. Few visitors made it to Lower, though there were exceptions; Three more lads from Liverpool arrived one morning (why are they always from Liverpool?), asking where they could buy some dry socks as they poured the water out of their boots. Their dedication was rewarded within moments though, when they picked up an otter swimming very fast along the edge of the reedbed. It remained mostly underwater, showing itself only intermittently, and left behind a wake like that of a small torpedo!

This was also the year when I first began monitoring the little egret roost at Leighton Moss, a role I stepped into fairly easily since I was already visiting the reserve at the appropriate times of day. I did have my priorities though, so when otters were showing the egret count had to wait.

Water levels began to fall in late February, and so did the temperature. Ice began to form on the water, and by the middle of the month the reserve was completely frozen. A fox was curled up, asleep, on the bank in the right-hand corner of Lower pool, apparently oblivious to the cold.

As the year progressed I often saw the female otter and her two cubs, sometimes together, and sometimes apart, but the cubs were so well grown by now that size differences were very difficult to discern in the water. When the three otters swam alongside each other they could appear to be of similar proportions, yet at other times the leading animal might seem larger when the other two were porpoising behind. The latter observation when the cubs were younger could safely be interpreted as a mother and cubs, but caution needs to be exercised as the cubs grow. Dog otter cubs in family groups can be bigger than their mother, so a group of otters with any larger individuals could include a mixed sex group of cubs, with or without their mother.

Otters showed themselves more frequently this year, and visitors increasingly reported seeing them in daylight. I came across otter tracks in the mud on nearby Silverdale Moss, so there were otters there too, though of unknown origin.

The reserve flooded again in October, and I resumed wading down Lower path, where shoals of small fish had now taken up residence. Their silvery scales glinted in the winter sun as they scattered at my approach.

A single otter was diving and fishing in Lower pool. Coots and ducks watched apprehensively from the Spit, as a second otter joined it. The two animals lingered in the bay towards the back of the pool, unsettling the wildfowl by their presence, but never coming quite near enough to panic them. They seemed to be enjoying having the place to themselves, and boxed playfully for a while whenever they came close to each other. Eventually the coots and ducks returned to the water, perhaps fed up of waiting for the otters to leave?

At the end of November temperatures plummeted, bringing overnight snow.

I hurried to Lower hide, where I saw an otter crossing the ice in front of Big island. Suddenly it stopped and pounced, like a polar bear hunting seals. It repeatedly hurled itself at the surface until eventually it managed to break through, and then disappeared and was gone. Fantastic!

The big freeze persisted until the end of February 2009. Contractors then moved in to dig out accumulated silt from the main reserve, as part of a large-scale project to improve the condition of the reedbed. The work continued until September and involved the daily use of heavy plant and industrial pumping systems. I continued my monitoring throughout this period, but saw few otters, so it seemed that perhaps they were staying out of the way.

By October 2009 the contractors had gone, and it was remarkable just how quickly the reserve recovered. I began to spend more time in Lower hide again, enjoying the wonderful light of early autumn, as the sun set over the reedbed. One evening, just before dusk, birds flew out from Island Mere in panic, filling the air with their alarm calls. There were no raptors to be seen, so I wondered whether otters in Island Mere pool might be the cause of the disturbance, or maybe this was just wishful thinking on my part? Then my suspicions were confirmed, as an otter emerged from the inlet. It only came a short distance into Lower pool before it turned towards the back edge and into the reeds. I focused my scope on the calm water and scanned the whole area, eager to find the animal again. I could hear greylag geese cackling noisily as they took flight from the back channel, but I ignored them and concentrated on the surface of the water. There was movement by the reed edge. An otter appeared, only this time it was not alone, and I was thrilled to see two smaller heads breaking the water close behind. The three animals made their way towards the Border, in a close-knit group, the mother leading the way. My second litter at Leighton Moss, a little more than two years after the first, welcome news that so many had been hoping for.

I made numerous attempts over the next few weeks to see the new cubs again, to no avail, but the walk back down Lower hide path was always worthwhile at this time of year.

I often heard the distinctive trilling of redpolls, which favoured the very tops of the alder trees, often in the company of siskins, which would hang upside down as they fed on the seeds. The treecreeper's call, inaudibly high for some listeners, would alert me to the presence of this woodland specialist, as it dropped from one tree to spiral up the next, its fluorescent white belly making a mockery of its cryptic camouflage.

Temperatures nosedived in December, and one late afternoon I sat in Lower hide listening to the sounds of ice breaking on the far side of the pool. Scanning the back edge of the reeds, I could see an otter popping up through the thin ice to take a breath, only its head showing above the water. Over the next twenty minutes it disappeared and reappeared again and again, but it was a hard act to follow, with only the cracking sounds to alert me each time it briefly surfaced.

The reserve remained frozen until the end of January 2010, and otters put in few appearances, though there were still signs of them in the form of spraint, and prints in the snow.

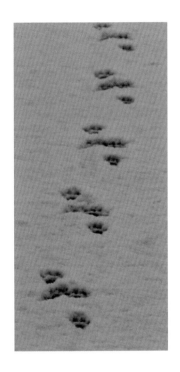

After weeks of frozen conditions the reserve finally thawed as February arrived, and one evening at dusk I watched a single otter diving to the left of Big island. It caught a fish and carried it towards the back channel. This performance was repeated several times, then three otters swam out and dived around Big island, but it was difficult to tell them apart whilst they were in the water.

Fortuitously, however, an overnight freeze brought the return of the ice, and the following evening all three otters walked across it in full view. I could now easily see that there was a mature female followed by two smaller individuals. It had been four months since I first glimpsed the two cubs, and if these were the same animals, which seemed likely, then they would now be around 7 to 8 months old, which would be consistent with their size.

One very cold evening in February I was joined by three young RSPB volunteers looking for their first otter. We soon found one, fishing on the Border, in one of the few unfrozen areas. It came out onto the ice, and ran right along the edge of the pool and into the reeds. It was getting dark and even colder, but the young people were not going to give up, and nor was I, despite encroaching hypothermia! Then, with the frosty white conditions illuminating the oncoming dusk, we saw three otters struggling through the thin ice at the reed edge. The stronger female in front repeatedly tried to climb up onto the ice, but at each thrust forward the ice broke beneath her. She paused often, waiting for the youngsters to catch up, before they finally made it onto the thicker ice behind Big island. We had all forgotten the cold by then.

At the end of the month a single otter was taking small prey and eating it, before finally catching a large eel and carrying it off to the reeds. Shortly thereafter the female returned with both cubs, and over the next half hour I watched her repeatedly catch small eels and drop them in front of the young otters. They squabbled over each of the gifts, and I realised that I was watching a fishing lesson. The female caught another large eel and began to swim back towards the reeds with one cub chasing, trying to dive over and take it from her. Moments later I saw the second cub on Big island, holding down an eel it must have caught and carried there, so clearly the lesson had been a success. The eel escaped though, and the otter cub returned to the water, looking somewhat bemused.

A few weeks later I saw the cubs again, in front of Lower hide. One began to head towards the bank with a fish, and as it did so a heron flew past the window and landed where it thought the otter would come out. On seeing the heron the otter swam on a little further, then brought the fish ashore. It dropped its catch and ran at the heron to push it aside, before reclaiming its breakfast and carrying it off into the reeds. The heron began to follow, but was startled by the second otter climbing out of the water and jumping straight in front of it. A game then followed, with the cubs appearing to amuse themselves at the heron's expense. They peeped out through the reeds until the heron came close enough for them to spring out and take it by surprise, then returned to the reedbed in order to repeat the trick.

Tired of this intimidation the heron flew off, leaving the young otters to enjoy their meal, and I saw no more of them that morning.

The family remained together through the spring and into summer, and I saw them frequently, but it became increasingly difficult to tell them apart on the basis of size, suggesting that both cubs were females. All three were very actively diving and catching prey for themselves, which almost always consisted of eels, some of them quite enormous.

Chapter Two

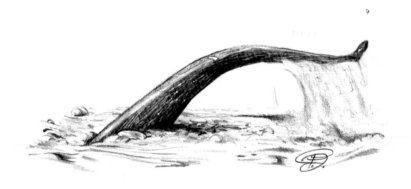

One evening in early August I watched an otter that was fishing close in front of Lower hide for quite some time. As it dived I could see not only how very large and powerful it was, but also that it had a curious kink in the end of its huge tail, which had a very thick muscular base. This was in keeping with the physique of the rest of the animal, which I was sure must be a dog otter. It swam into the right-hand pool, scattering flightless ducks, as it very obligingly gave me even more time to have a good look at the tail, which was clearly either a deformity or a healed injury, rather than simply the way it was being held. I was thus able to individualise an otter for the first time, and I had no doubt that I would easily be able to recognise this animal if I saw it again.

The following evening it was raining, but I thought it would only be a shower, and as it was cloudy it seemed a good opportunity to count the little egrets in to roost earlier, as they tended to arrive sooner in darker conditions. By the time I got to Lower hide the shower had turned into a real downpour and the egrets had already started to arrive. I never did count them though ...

Two otters came out of the reeds to the left of Big island. One of them was the kinky-tailed individual seen the day before, whilst the second was noticeably less muscular and obviously smaller. They writhed around each other, often submerging, and the larger otter was seen to hold the other by the scruff of the neck and push it underwater. I had extremely good views of all this since they remained in the same spot for over twenty minutes and I was able to zoom in on full magnification. The exchange was noticeably one-sided, the larger animal held the other by the neck, but there was no attempt at any sort of retaliation by the other, as you see when cubs are play fighting. They reeled and rolled together in a way I had never seen before, in very close contact, and I realised that what I was witnessing was copulation. At the end of the liaison the two parted and went their separate ways. The smaller one retired into the reeds, but Kinky tail stayed out in the open and fished for another fifteen minutes or so.

Confirmation that Kinky was a male, together with the ability to recognise him individually, would later provide important lessons on the difficulties of sexing otters in the field. A full grown female Eurasian otter on mainland Britain measures about 1.0 m from nose to tail tip and weighs around 7 kg, whilst a large male can measure up to 1.2 m and weigh around 10 kg. Males are also often said to have broader heads than females, though recent research casts doubt upon this as a useful field aid. In theory then, otters can be sexed on the basis of size and muscularity, and over my ten years of observations I met many people who purported to do this with confidence and ease, and who had no apparent difficulty in proclaiming the sex of a distant otter from a mere glimpse.

However, because size and distance are always relative this can make it impossible to be sure of the exact dimensions of an animal without any nearby features to compare it with.

At close quarters, as in the copulation event above, comparisons could be made fairly easily, although the presence of a larger and a smaller animal would more usually indicate a mother and cub rather than a male and female, but in the case of lone otters swimming at distance absolute estimates of their stature are all but impossible.

Kinky provided perfect illustrations of this because on a number of occasions when I saw him at distance in the water there was nothing to suggest that he was unusually large or muscular, and I was able to identify him only when I had sight of his tail. On other occasions I saw what did appear to be particularly large otters disappearing into the reedbed, only to then see them reappear moments later with cubs.

Sometimes the only way to be absolutely certain of the sex of an otter is to see it urinating, which males do forwards and females backwards, but I never once saw this at Leighton Moss in ten years of trying.

Three nights later I again saw Kinky, who spent twenty minutes cruising and fishing along the back of Lower pool, but with no other otters in sight.

The following morning I called into Lower hide taking only my binoculars, as I had intended only a brief visit. A disturbance near Big island alerted me to an otter, appearing surprisingly small without my scope. I then picked up a second animal near the Border, which was heading straight for the first otter at breakneck speed.

They clashed in a ferocious and noisy confrontation, vocalising loudly as they bit and clawed at each other in a serious brawl.

The bout ended when one otter fled, with the other pursuing it into the reeds far right of Lower hide. The swimming was so fast and powerful that when they leapt out of the water their bodies were almost horizontal, instead of the more usual curved dive, and they looked more like flying fish than otters. At the speed they were moving, and with only my binoculars, it wasn't possible to see if one of them was Kinky.

Over the next month I had three more sightings of Kinky, twice on his own and once in the company of a smaller animal, and in mid-September I had a very memorable experience.

It was a beautiful calm morning. A ripple crossed the still water towards Big island, and two black terns dipped into it. An otter surfaced. It was Kinky. He made two more dives to the edge of the reeds and was gone. Only the terns were now disturbing their mirror images. A few moments later a whirlpool of water drew my attention to a second otter behind the three posts. It turned towards the hide, and I held my breath as it came even closer. I could see the shine of its wet fur, and the droplets of water falling from its whiskers were clearly visible even without binoculars, as it dived powerfully again and again.

The two young volunteers who had said they were going to come should have set their alarm ...

It was worthy of note that during all of the recent otter activity there had been no spraint at all on the causeway.

The hide was quite full that same evening due to the otters showing so well lately, but most people gave up as dusk fell. Shortly after, as the first egrets began to arrive, two otters spilled out from behind Big island, porpoising powerfully out of the water. A tangle then took place of thrashing bodies, tails and bared teeth, one set of which belonged to Kinky. The fight, clearly in earnest, was viciously contested, but Kinky soon gained the advantage and the second otter fled towards the back edge near Otter island. Kinky remained diving to the right of Big island and then began to swim towards the hide. On a final dive just past the posts he pulled off the all too familiar otter Houdini routine, and vanished without trace.

When otters are hunting they usually stay underwater for only 20 to 30 seconds, and employ a 'patch fishing' technique, where they dive and surface repeatedly in the same area. If necessary, however, they can remain submerged for up to 90 seconds, and as they are capable of swimming underwater at about 1.5 metres per second they can travel a considerable distance in that time. I have very often seen the wake of an underwater otter cross from one side of the pool to the other without even a glimpse of the animal itself. It cannot be assumed that a diving otter will resurface anywhere near where it went down, and I soon learned the importance of scanning widely when tracking them.

The next day, in heavy rain, I watched a lone black-headed gull, swooping, it seemed, at the raindrops. But it wasn't. It was following an otter that was fishing along the back edge. It turned towards the posts, and dived again. It was Kinky.

A visitor in the hide, who was sporting full camouflage gear and had enough camera equipment for a David Attenborough assignment, explained that he was an otter expert who ran four day workshops on Mull, teaching people about sea otters, which came as some surprise to me since to the best of my knowledge this is a colonial species whose nearest haunt is in California. Perhaps I would like to go on one of his courses, he wondered?

He drew my attention to the otter now fishing in the far right-hand corner, diving quite powerfully, which he confidently informed me was a young otter.

'Adult, I think,' I suggested.

My use of the word 'think', intended as politeness rather than uncertainty, was obviously not a good choice since this encouraged him to regale me with accounts of the hundreds of otter photos he had taken, which quite clearly showed the paler underbelly that is (apparently) characteristic of young otters. He could also tell that it was a youngster by the way it swam and dived …

'Have you read Kruuk?' I asked, as tolerantly as I could, as my patience was wearing a little thin. 'No? Gosh, I am surprised, you seem to know so much.'

Professor Hans Kruuk is the pre-eminent UK authority on otter research, and his review on the subject, cited in my acknowledgements, is essential reading for anyone with a serious interest in these animals.

In the preface to his book, Kruuk points out that the appeal of otters to the general public has fostered a wealth of popular writing, mostly by naturalists, in books, magazines and unrefereed journals. These are generally referred to by scientists, somewhat condescendingly, as the 'grey literature'. Whilst these sources may contain excellent and useful observations, he cautions that they often require a large dose of salt and that it can be difficult to extract the good information from the bad or the merely entertaining.

My own writings obviously form part of this same grey literature, but rely entirely on Kruuk regarding otter ecology and behaviour, rather than on any of the greyer sources which informed so many of the wildlife experts I have encountered during my time at Leighton Moss.

There was a short pause in the conversation in the hide, after which this particular expert volunteered that the writings of a well-known TV naturalist and cameraman were his principal source of information, and that he could tell it was a young otter by the distinctive shape of its head.

I wondered whether perhaps he might like to hear about one or two of my own special moments, but resisted the temptation as I had already learnt more than enough for one day.

As October progressed, with water levels still quite high, four great-crested grebes cruised around Lower pool, their heads held under the water as they searched for prey. At distance this behaviour can provide a very convincing otter impersonation for the unwary and so always warrants close inspection.

A heron, which all morning had remained stock still just at the water's edge outside the hide, suddenly made a stab into the shallow pool and pulled out a huge pike, dragging it onto the bank. It then proceeded to inflict further damage by repeatedly driving its lower mandible into the flesh of its victim, until finally the fish lay still. I could not believe that a fish of that size would fit down the heron's throat. Nevertheless, it opened its bill, took the pike by the head, and proceeded to lift it into swallowing position. It stood like this for some time, with only the head of the over-sized prey in its gullet. The fish was finally abandoned, and the heron walked to the water's edge and washed the blood from its bill.

I was glad that watching the heron had kept me there that morning, when the coots scuttled out from the Bittern post, and almost immediately an otter appeared. It proceeded to head towards the reeds at the back of the pool, with an eel in its mouth. I noted that although it did not look as though it had far to swim from where it had caught the prey to the back edge of the pool, it still took quite some time to get there. This was another good demonstration of how difficult it can be to accurately estimate distances, and therefore sizes, across an expanse of featureless water, an observation that I would repeat many times over the years.

By morning the pike had gone. Kinky was cruising behind the posts, with another otter alongside. After a few moments they split up and fished apart. In the background, I witnessed a third otter moving quickly from the Spit and across the back edge of the pool.

Recent reports had mostly been of only single otters, which was unsurprising, because otter sightings are so thrilling that the natural tendency for most observers is to watch the animal they have found until it disappears from view. Few people turn from the sighting they already have in order to scan the empty water for another one, so visitors will often see only single otters simply because they aren't looking for any more.

Towards the end of October temperatures started to fall, bringing frosty conditions, which usually precipitated the start of the red deer rut. One morning around a hundred little egrets left the roost, and two waves of starlings flew out as the sun lit the woods around the mere.

A dense mist began to roll over the water, while a great white egret stalked the shallows close to the hide. I left, as I was so cold, and walked down the path, where a magnificent red deer stag bellowed from the edge of the reedbed.

On a beautiful, but very cold, November morning, with ice all round the shallow edges of the water, I watched from Lower hide, as the winter sun peered feebly over the treetops.

Two new volunteers had joined me, and we did not have long to wait before I located a wake heading right from the Spit, immediately followed by a second ripple behind Big island, leading under the ice. The volunteers were surprised at how quickly I had found, and then lost, the otters, without their seeing anything at all, but then I had the advantage of knowing where to look!

I directed them to the spit edge, where they shared their first otter encounter, which was Kinky, and it was a treat for me to see him too, since I hadn't done so for almost two weeks. The second otter swam towards the Border and was lost to view.

'That made my day!' said one of the volunteers.

Freezing temperatures brought the first snowfall of the winter at the end of November, and low water levels meant that Leighton froze very quickly. I hurried to the reserve to take full advantage of the weather before any tracks or signs were disturbed.

I found otter prints in the snow on the east side of the causeway, and fresh spraint, which was arranged in two piles, one on either side of the bridge. These were of quite different appearance and texture, indicating the presence of at least two animals.

Arctic conditions continued at Leighton, and by Christmas Eve the pools had been frozen for a month, apart from a small patch of open water at Causeway hide.

Overnight snow revealed large otter prints on the west side of Causeway bridge, and a very small amount of fresh spraint, but there were no prints on the east side. This was reversed the next day, when there were smaller prints on the east side, and broken ice under the bridge. I saw no more otter signs after this until the start of January 2011, when once again I began to find spraint.

Otter spraint is scented by secretions from the otters' anal glands and has a characteristic odour, often described as that of newly mown hay, which is unmistakable and not at all unpleasant. Otters deposit spraint at favourite locations in order to indicate their presence to other otters, and since it contains remains of the prey consumed by the animals it can also provide limited evidence of their diet. Paradoxically, young otters often deposit large amounts of spraint, whilst mature dog otters leave the smallest deposits, maybe because they better appreciate its value and therefore use it more sparingly.

Towards the end of January I found anal jelly deposited on the rocks at Causeway bridge, but still I saw no otters.

This jelly usually forms a lining to otter intestines, protecting them from damage by sharp fish bones, but Kruuk reports that when captive otters have not fed for a day or more then this jelly is excreted in place of normal spraint. This too is anointed by the anal glands, and so bears the same characteristic odour as normal spraint, but the reason for its production is not elimination of food remains.

On an unseasonably warm morning at the start of February a party of lapwings called evocatively as they flew over the Spit, their premature display a welcoming herald of the coming spring. I too shared their eagerness for the new season, and on that day it felt all the closer for the brief performance.

I saw a single otter diving to the right of Big island the next day. This was my first for almost three months, and even though I had known they were around throughout the winter, it was good to actually see one again.

Otters continued to show well, and I saw two or three almost every day, cruising the usual areas and catching plenty of prey, mostly eels. There was, however, no sign of Kinky, and I wondered if he was still around.

In late February, two otters of similar size appeared on the Border, and over the course of the next five minutes they gradually moved towards the front of Big island.

One began to head towards the hide carrying a large eel, but just before reaching the shore it turned towards the Bittern post and hauled itself out of the water. It began chewing the head of the unfortunate fish, and I could hear the crunching sounds in the still morning air.

Suddenly the second otter leapt out and grabbed the other end of the squirming prey. A brief tussle ensued before the thief gained the upper hand and won itself an easy meal, which it quickly chewed and swallowed to put an end to any argument. Both otters then returned to the pool and continued to fish independently.

Two or three otters were seen regularly throughout March and April, but still there was no sign of Kinky. Then, on a rainy and windy day in the middle of May, an otter was diving behind the posts. The animal had a particular presence, and exuded a certain air of familiarity, but showed tantalisingly little of itself above water.

Finally, as it came nearer to the hide and surfaced ever so briefly I glimpsed the peculiar bend in his tail, and my spirits soared. Kinky was back!

As the days grew longer, and spring gave way to summer, the reserve was once more filled with the familiar sounds of breeding birds. The years spent learning all their songs and calls always brought rewards at this time of year, when many of the inhabitants of the reedbed were more often heard than seen.

In June there was an eruption of blue-tailed damselflies, and many hundreds of them gathered along the causeway. The flag iris was in bloom all around the water's edge, and the bright blue insects swarmed around their yellow flowers.

I had now been studying otters at Leighton Moss on a near daily basis for over five years, and had learnt much, whilst enjoying some phenomenal spectacles. Nothing, however, could have prepared me for the events that followed, which would throw Leighton Moss into the spotlight of the local media, drawing large numbers of expectant visitors.

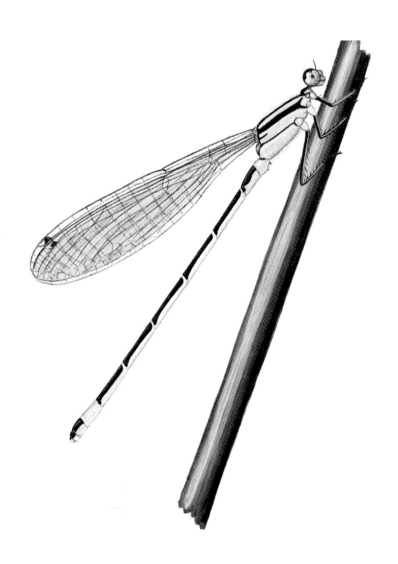

Chapter Three

The first three mornings in August I had cycled to the wader pools and enjoyed stunning views of a green sandpiper, but heavy rain was forecast and my bicycle needed some repair, so I walked to Lower hide instead.

The rain began to pelt down, but there was no wind, so I opened the window and surveyed the scene. There were a good many birds on the water, seemingly unperturbed by the downpour, and everything seemed serene.

Then, suddenly, a couple of mallards flew up from the Border. They had been flighty for the last couple of weeks for no obvious reason, but old habits of checking just in case made me scan the reed edge, and I picked up what I can only describe as a bubbling cauldron of otters! Legs, tails and heads were writhing together and pouring out of the reeds in one mass. Moments later a larger otter split from the group and began to swim left, and porpoising right behind were not one, or two, but three smaller individuals. I was overjoyed to see new cubs again, and impressed by their number, since both the previous families had contained only two cubs each.

They did not travel far before they turned and went back into the reeds. A single otter, which I presumed to be the mother, was fishing on the Border later, but I saw no more of the cubs that morning.

I, of course, returned at dusk.

John Wilson arrived with his grandson Sam, as I had told him earlier of my latest discovery, and he presented me with an award for my endeavours, in the form of a courgette from his allotment.

Thanks John, though I've never really regarded them as edible, so I'll need to think of something suitably creative to do with it. Even a humble vegetable from the likes of the legendary John Wilson is an honour indeed, and I shall treasure it, though obviously not for very long, such is the fate of perishable accolades ...

There were other people in the hide, clicking their cameras at a heron.

I spotted an adult otter to the right of Big island, but there was no sign of any cubs. John pointed out the otter to the visitors and, as they all enjoyed watching it, I scanned the rest of the pool in search of the three young.

The light was beginning to fade and we had now lost sight of the lone individual. People began to leave as the little egrets started to drop into the roost, and hope of a repeat of this morning's events began to dim. I was just about to pack up and go myself, when one last scan revealed otters swimming right from Big island. All eyes were fixed on the group trying to see how many there were.

They began to head towards a newly cut area on the far back edge, and we realised that there was a possibility they might climb out, and sure enough, this is exactly what happened. There was much scurrying about in and out of the reeds at first, before they settled down. It was then noted that the larger female otter was huddled up closely to not one, but two cubs, which hadn't been apparent at first, whilst a third lay a short way off, eating a fish.

Three cubs were confirmed then.

The group remained on the bank for a couple of minutes and we had absolutely fabulous views, at least as good as I'd ever seen. At one point one of the cubs approached the one with the fish, making an unsuccessful challenge, which was repelled with bared teeth. They finally slid back into the pool and swam off into the gloom, and we were left spellbound at the mesmerising event we had all just shared.

Two of the cubs were in the pool to the right of Lower hide the next evening, and to my great delight they both left the water. Their sleek coats glistened as they chased each other up and down the bank, before splashing back into the pool. The chase continued along the water's edge until they climbed out once again, and bounded off into the reeds.

After a week without any further sightings of the mother and cubs, I decided to make it to Lower hide just as the sun was rising. The little egrets were already leaving the roost and sand martins were snatching aerial prey over the water.

Around thirty little egrets landed on the Spit, much to the annoyance of the juvenile great black-backed gull. Splashing on the far back edge drew my attention, and I saw that there were two small otters play fighting. I zoomed in for a better look, just in time to watch them go back into the reeds. I scanned the rest of the reedbed, as a bittern had recently been reported, all the while keeping an eye out for more otters.

The morning wore on, and as it grew lighter, parties of ducks began dropping in as the rest of the little egrets flew out west. There was a commotion in Causeway pool, and as the coots scattered I saw an otter swimming quite purposefully towards Big island, carrying a large fish. The size and strength of the animal suggested it was most likely the female returning. The otter continued on past the island towards the back edge and swam into the reeds just where I had seen the two cubs enter earlier. I waited and watched.

For quite a while nothing happened, then, scanning around, I spotted two otter cubs to the right of Otter island. I looked towards the Border where I saw there was another otter fishing by itself. Back to the two together, but now there were three of similar size tumbling around in a tight ball.

'OK,' I thought, 'I shall enjoy watching the cubs.'

As I watched, a larger individual approached them, so I had four otters now, with a fifth lone animal still fishing on the Border; yes, it was still there. The three cubs continued encircling each other, but close to the side of them the larger one was now coiling around another youngster, so I now had five together, with the sixth still fishing apart from them.

Keeping as calm as I could, I re-counted what had now become a whole pack of otters. It was quite easy to do as the group of three remained slightly apart from the other two. All five began to head towards the hide, arriving at the end of the reeds less than ten metres away from me. I had all of them in my scope at the same time, an unforgettable sight that I could never have anticipated. Then they were gone, as if the whole encounter had been a dream. I looked back towards the Border, and the sixth otter was still there.

The only possible interpretation of the intimate group of five was that it was a mother and cubs, so it transpired that the female actually had four young. Not unheard of – Eurasian otters can have up to five – but certainly very unusual, and probably indicative of the quality of feeding resources available on the reserve. The sixth otter was most likely a female from another core territory, since it kept itself apart from the family of five, but did not experience any hostility from the mother of the cubs.

Female otters each hold a core territory, which is where they spend around half of their time, and where they rear their young. Core territories of related females are adjacent to each other, in a group territory, over which the females will range for the rest of their time, though staying well out of each other's way. Related females will sometimes visit each other's core areas without any display of aggression, but females from outside the group territory are forcibly excluded.

Female group territories are fairly stable, but core territories may change from one year to the next, not least because of otters' surprisingly low life expectancy. In Shetland, Kruuk found that females were resident in core areas for an average of only 2 years, after which they disappeared and were assumed to have died.

Male otters, in contrast to females, have huge ranges that overlap with several female group territories. Each male range is used by several males simultaneously, which avoid making any contact with each other, but when chance meetings do occur they are almost always very aggressive indeed.

The next morning I walked to Lower hide through the fields overlooking Leighton Moss. A female roe deer, accompanied by two young, stood at the top of the hill looking down at me. I was glad I had decided to take the longer route as I watched the mist roll over the pools on the reserve. Swallows gathered in migratory numbers on the wires by Grisedale farm, and the kestrel perched in its usual spot at the edge of the woods.

I reached the hide as the last of the mist lifted. Other people entered, and we all sat in silence and looked out over the pool. There was a disturbance to the right of the Spit on the far back edge. I did not say anything until I was on them, and then my heart leapt as I saw a cluster of bodies and tails, though the birds in the water around them paid little attention. With my help the rest of the people in the hide were now on to them too, and we all enjoyed counting the group as they alternately split apart and coiled around each other. There were four, all of similar size. They played together for quite some time, providing excellent views, then went into the inlet. Some of the people in the hide had never seen an otter before, let alone four, and they were understandably enchanted.

I made what I thought was a very early start the day after, but the egrets appeared to have already left by the time I arrived. Two loud shots rang out, courtesy of the deer stalker, which confirmed that all of the little egrets had indeed already gone, since no more flew out. A single otter was making its way towards Big island, so I scanned the rest of the pool, but could see no others. I continued watching the same area, as a pattern of seeing a single otter followed by the appearance of cubs had been apparent on more than one occasion of late.

Five cormorants dropped in and began to fish, only instead of diving they swam about in a compact group, dipping their heads under the water and coming up with tiny silver fish in their bills, which they tossed and swallowed. Another two flew in and joined them, and all seven swirled around in front of the hide, dipping their heads one after another as though the performance had been rehearsed.

Three goosanders flew out of the far back channel, and I wondered if something had spooked them?

I could see nothing at first, but the remaining birds on the Spit were all staring in the same direction as me! I felt a bit of a cheat, as I did not tell the couple who were in the hide with me what I thought was about to happen, but you can never be sure. A ripple spread out from the channel, then another.

'Otters on the back edge,' I exclaimed, as I saw two tails go down.

The couple began to count excitedly, as once again an entangled ball of otters split and joined in a playful group.

'Three, no, four,' they decided.

They were right. We followed the four otters as they headed directly for the Spit, where surely they were going to climb out? Two of them did so briefly, sending the remaining mallards into a complete frenzy. They slipped back into the shallow water, rejoining the other two, and as the four of them splashed around inquisitively in the same area, I was able to zoom in and see that they were catching small eels and chewing them, one even managing to catch its own tail!

Then they were off, racing down the reed edge left of Big island, slipping in and out of the reeds more like eels themselves than otters. As they reached the spot where I had seen them enter on previous days they again drew tightly together. It was then I realised that one seemed a little larger, surely there were now five? The mother must have joined them. Then, as I tried to confirm the count, the group split apart.

'One is swimming away,' the couple announced.

The larger otter had left the group and was heading towards the Border.

'Please keep your eyes on that one,' I said, 'While I re-count the others.'

It did not take long; 'One, two three, four,' they were easy to count as they were well apart from each other in the open water. The couple had kept their eyes on the female otter, which was now fishing on the Border.

Her four cubs would require twice as much feeding as previous litters of only two, which perhaps explained the increased frequency of otter reports by visitors to the reserve, yet I noted that there had been no spraint on the Causeway bridge for over three weeks.

The next day brought more activity, beginning with a single otter that arrived from the direction of Causeway pool. As it approached Big island it submerged, and I followed its wake round the island and out of sight.

A group of visitors arrived, and began to talk, somewhat disparagingly, about a report put out by the RSPB that 'some woman' had reported seeing five otters! I smiled to myself, and scanned all the usual spots.

To the left of Big Island a group of otters milled about on the surface, surely no one could miss these? I said nothing, and left the visitors to count for themselves.

'Definitely more than one,' a lady announced confidently. 'Maybe three?'

I focused intently on the group. There were four.

The visitors argued amongst themselves for a little while, but eventually they too concluded that there were indeed four.

A larger individual had now joined the tumbling bodies. I remained silent and held my breath waiting for them to split.

'Three going right now,' I had to spurt out, 'I'm following them, how many are still there?'

A shout of 'Two!' rang out.

Then, as the three swimming to the right came porpoising back to join the remaining two, I revelled in the fact that once again I had been fortunate enough to have shared this incredible sight, a female otter with four cubs. The otters remained around the island for over half an hour, play fighting and swimming in and out of the reeds. I was able to easily pick out the female as she was usually the leader of the group, and at one point I actually saw all four cubs leap right on top of her.

We continued watching, engrossed in the behaviour of the young otters, when all at once the spellbinding moment was broken as a real pandemonium erupted from the right-hand pool. All the ducks took to the air and coots scuttled around the edge of the reeds.

A huge wake appeared, just past the Bittern post, and an otter surfaced, then gave such a slap of its tail that the waves it made ran on past the hide. It dived repeatedly. This was obviously an impressive specimen, and, although at first I could not be certain, I fancied there was a familiar irregularity in its tail. Captivated by the possibility that I might be seeing Kinky once again, I quickly checked to see if the otter family were still by the island, but they were nowhere to be seen.

The otter began swimming and diving more slowly, and I could now conclusively see the very distinctive kink. I was quite overwhelmed to see this otter again, as I hadn't seen him for over three months. I told the visitors in the hide that this morning's experience had by far surpassed any other, apart from that misty morning when I came across my first otter.

Yet more drama awaited me on my next visit to Lower. As I watched, an enormous fish leapt right out of the water, and fell back in with a huge splash. It fled for its life across the pool, with an otter in hot pursuit, and all the while I could see the wake of the fish just under the water, and sometimes its muscular body as it broke the surface. It twisted and turned and changed direction, desperately trying to shake off its nemesis, but to no avail. The otter was determined not to lose this one and, like a cheetah pursuing a gazelle, it continued the chase until its quarry made a wrong turning and was caught. The otter struggled to subdue the fish, and when it was finally brought to the surface I could see that it was a pike, of potentially record-breaking proportions. The otter half-carried, half-dragged its prey into the reeds to the right of the hide. Breakfast for the growing cubs?

The next day I spent three hours in the hide , but no otters appeared, and there was no spraint on the Causeway bridge. This was to be my last visit for a week, but I hoped the otters would show again on my return.

Chapter Four

Whilst I was away there had been heavy rain, and water levels were very high, which often seems to increase the chance of seeing otters, but for my first three days back I had no luck.

I was up before the bats came home the morning after, as I wanted to count the little egrets out of the roost, and I arrived just in time to see them take to the air.

A water rail squealed, and as I glanced down to see if it was going to come out into the open I saw a small otter paddling along the wet bank, in and out of the reed edge towards the Bittern post. As I watched the young otter I heard a high-pitched whistle. The cub was calling. A few moments later a second cub arrived, and they made their way to the water, one slightly ahead and constantly whistling.

They swam belly flop style, with heads held up above the water, across the pool towards Island Mere. Two more joined them, and they converged before weaving their way through the tree roots at the entrance to the inlet.

It was now mid-September. As I made my way to Lower hide it began to rain, though thankfully the high winds, which had blown all night, had now dropped considerably. A gentleman who was there when I arrived said he had been watching otters for twenty minutes and had managed to count four, though not all at the same time.

I counted three straight away, with a fourth swimming determinedly towards them from the direction of the Border. It joined the other three and they all began to dive almost as one, heads, bodies and tails disappearing in constant perpetual motion. As they remained in more or less the same area I was able to zoom in, and could see that on occasion one or other would surface, chewing something it had caught. One rolled over, grasping a small fish with its claws, and I managed several times to see small eels held firmly between their teeth. There was no evidence of any of them catching anything more substantial, so presumably their mother was still also feeding them.

Suddenly they stopped diving, and began to swim with bounding leaps towards the right of the pool, almost as though they had heard some sort of signal. As they reached the end of the reeds in front of the hide there was a swirl of bodies, and it was difficult to see exactly what was happening. Then the group turned and headed out towards the middle of the pool, leaping over each other as they went. There were five. They all resumed diving around the cormorant posts, going down over and over again. I tried to see If I could make out any size differences, but with their constant motion it was very difficult, though one did appear to lead with the others following after it.

They continued fishing and we were treated to the most exceptional views as they moved in front of the posts, often diving in synchrony. The group eventually broke up and headed off in single file towards the end of the reeds. We thought they must surely be about to leave the water for a rest, but on closer inspection we could see that one otter was grasping an enormous eel and the others were following after it. We lost sight of them for a few moments, and wondered if they were sharing this hearty catch, but four were soon back in the water where they continued to fish, so perhaps the female was having her own meal for once?

On a calm dry day at the end of September I left the house at first light, as I had not seen the family of five otters for two weeks. The sun rose above the hill and gradually illuminated the reed bed, and it was not difficult to be patient on this particular morning as I listened to bearded tits pinging through the reeds, and watched a juvenile marsh harrier flush the ducks from the Spit.

I scanned the water for otters for some time with no success, then, just as I was about to leave, small waves started to emanate from the left-hand edge of the Border and something dived. Even though I had not seen a tail I remarked to a visitor in the hide that I thought there was an otter, so certain was I.

At first there were just bubbles on the water, then two otters broke the surface and dived, tails in full view. Two more swam out, and then another, and I was elated to see the whole group swimming with heads up, breaking through the still water like scissors through silk.

They made their way to the reeds by Big island and wove in and out along the reed edge. Over the next half hour they split up and fished independently, and I saw no more than two at once for the rest of that morning. It was to be almost another three weeks before I saw them again as a family group.

September ended with a warm spell that continued into October, and an algal bloom covered most of the water. I saw no more than three otters at any one time, with most sightings being of only one or two.

There were increasing numbers of visitor reports of three otters play fighting later on in the day, and I wondered whether three of the cubs were now spending more time apart from their mother.

On a pleasant autumnal morning in mid-October I arrived in time to see a great white egret leave the roost. The little egrets jostled in the trees, leaving sporadically over the next hour. Flocks of redwings flew over, and parties of snipe were flushed by the three marsh harriers that still hunted on the reserve.

A group of teal took to the air as a sparrowhawk flew through, and a kingfisher called as it sped across the pool, leaving a trail of electric blue. A lady arrived and asked if I'd seen any otters, as she was on a quest for her first. She sat down and almost immediately saw ripples spreading out from Otter island, where we then had a tantalising glimpse of two otters. Beginner's luck …

Over the next few minutes we continued to watch, hoping that the two otters would reappear, and soon enough our wish was granted, when not two but three showed themselves. They took off to the right, but there was more to come, as two more followed them, and to my great joy they all climbed on to the cut area to the right of Otter island. I could see that the cubs were now quite a bit bigger than the first time I had seen them out of the water at the beginning of August, some ten weeks earlier. I also noted, for the first time, that one of the cubs was noticeably smaller than the other three.

By the end of October, the starling roost had swelled to about half a million birds, and their evening murmurations provided an astonishing spectacle. These were strikingly dramatic if a raptor, such as a peregrine, put in an appearance, as the starlings would produce amazing formations in their attempts to confuse the predator.

I watched in awe at Lower one morning as they left the roost *en masse*, providing a most exciting start to the day. The flock seemed to stretch from horizon to horizon, and as they flew over the hide their droppings peppered the surface of the pool, whilst the collective beating of their million wings sounded like a tropical rainstorm.

As I soaked up the tranquillity following their passage, a movement near Big island caught my eye, and the whole family of five otters appeared, with the female at the head of the group. She led them straight across the pool to disappear into the inlet at Island Mere, and they moved with a speed and urgency that I had never seen from them before.

Moments later the coots on the Border scattered and an otter surfaced.

It swam a little way towards the hide, and then dived. I had a good view of the tail, and saw that it was Kinky, whom I had not seen since the end of August, some two months earlier. I was certain that the female had seen him first this morning, and long before I had, which was why she had mustered the cubs and taken them into Island Mere.

The next morning I found fresh spraint on the Causeway bridge, but saw no otters despite being there for two hours after dawn, though a good view of a bittern made the wait worthwhile.

At the beginning of November three otters of similar size fished and chased each other, as one or other of them caught prey. It seemed that three of the cubs were now regularly fishing away from their mother, so they were showing evidence of becoming more independent.

Kinky cruised past Big island and along the back edge of the pool the next day, and although I didn't know it then, this was to be the last time I would ever see him.

The RSPB wardens spent the next week or so cutting the reeds around Lower hide and coppicing the trees along the path. I still made brief visits, but saw no otters, and by the time the work was finished it had been nine days since my last encounter. The weather was very mild, and water levels were dropping with the tip of the third post now visible.

The reeds which had been cut in front of the hide had been gathered into several small stacks, and as I looked out of the window I could hear a rustling sound coming from the nearest of them. I thought at first that it was a bird of some sort, but suddenly the head of a young stoat popped up, and glanced first one way then the other.

It came right out into the open, and stared back towards the stack, where the rustling continued.

A second stoat revealed itself, and the two then spent over half an hour chasing each other round and round and between the piles of reeds, leaping and bounding in a display of youthful exuberance.

I watched in amazement until finally they scampered off into the reedbed. I saw no otters that morning, but this had been one of my closest and most prolonged experiences ever of these elusive animals, and more than compensated for the absence of their larger cousins that day.

A good variety of ducks had joined the coots on the pool recently, and it was quite strange to see them so calm and relaxed after three months of almost daily disturbance by the otter family.

I was beginning to feel the onset of otter withdrawal symptoms, so I decided to make sure I arrived at Lower hide as soon as it was physically possible to see anything. Two woodcocks flew over my head on the way there, and I could hear the sound of starlings moving through the reed bed as I walked down the path to the hide. The little egrets had not yet left the roost, but a few black-headed gulls were in the air. I scanned the pool. Everything was just as it had been for the last few days.

Two sparrowhawks shot past the hide and the air was filled with the thunderous noise of thousands of starlings, as they whooshed out of their roost and span in great clouds along the tops of the reeds. Two marsh harriers flushed the little egrets, which flew in every direction around Island Mere, undecided perhaps as to whether it was too early to leave.

There was so much activity at Lower hide that morning that it came as no surprise when I saw two otters on the far back edge. None of the other occupants of the pool seemed to be taking any notice of them whatsoever, even when three more swam out from the channel to join them. They circled each other languidly, for no obvious purpose or reason, in marked contrast to the frenetic activity which had preceded their appearance. I was elated to see them again, even though it was a very distant view, and it wasn't long before they all went in to Island Mere.

Over the next couple of weeks visitors reported otters from Lower and Causeway hides, and also from Lilian's hide.

The following sketch shows the view from the Sky Tower next to Lilian's hide, looking eastwards, and though most of my observations were made from Lower and Causeway pools, these are only a short way from Lilian's, as the otter swims.

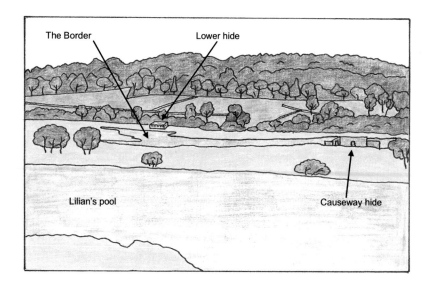

The beginning of December finally brought more settled weather, and although there was a slight frost it was not too cold. At least four otters had been reported going into Island Mere on the previous evening, so my hopes were high on my next visit. As I scanned the pool a movement to the left alerted me to an otter on the bank, which was carrying a large fish. Almost immediately two more joined it, but the first animal dived straight back into the water and headed towards the three posts. The other two stood motionless for only a moment before they set off in pursuit of the one with the fish.

As these three headed right the water swirled to the left of the hide and I watched as two more otters clambered ashore. One was larger than the other, and the smaller one was grappling with an eel it had caught, which it devoured before both otters dropped back into the water and headed for the middle of the pool. By now the other three were out of sight, to the right of the Bittern post.

The two in the middle of the pool began to swim towards Island Mere. One followed the other, and the lead animal, which was clearly the mother, held her head above the water giving short whistling calls. The three that had swum off returned to join them, now without the fish, and they all slipped one by one into the inlet.

This was turning out to be a really interesting scenario; the most plausible interpretation of my observations was that the three larger cubs were dog otters whilst the smaller one was a female. This conclusion was based as much on behaviour as on size difference, as the larger cubs showed growing confidence and independence, whilst the smaller one spent more time in the company of her mother.

The frequency of visitor sightings of late had led some to suggest that perhaps there were now two otter families at Leighton Moss. I was quite sure, however, that most accounts on the reserve were of this one family, which I had personally seen in all of the many different combinations that had been reported by others, and apart from infrequent appearances of Kinky I had only seen a second lone otter fishing near the group on one occasion.

Wild weather returned, and persisted throughout December, with high winds, heavy rain and frequent icy hail showers. Water levels rose and the paths began to flood, while falling temperatures brought overnight frosts and frozen surfaces on paths and water. Darkness often fell around mid-afternoon and visits were brief, though otters were still seen.

On a terribly wet and windy morning, about halfway through the month, I braved the elements to reach Lower hide. The water was very rough, and alternate rain and hail showers were lashing the windows on my arrival.

The coots were all crowding together, and a black-headed gull was the only bird in the air. It began mobbing something on the far right edge, and I scanned the choppy water to find that the object of its attention was a group of otters.

They repeatedly dived, vanishing momentarily, but each time they resurfaced they were coming just a little closer to the hide. As they did so I could see that all five were present, and that one of them had an eel wrapped around its head. It held on to it tenaciously, as the others, all wanting a share, leapt around snapping at it in a frenzied commotion, but the otter with the eel broke free and escaped with its prize.

The hail returned, bouncing off the windows so hard that it was impossible to see what was happening, and by the time it had stopped the otters were gone.

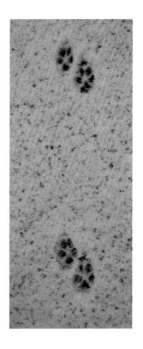

The wind and rain ceased a couple of days later, and it began to snow. I found fox prints along the path, but the snow on the causeway had thawed by the time I got there.

Leighton froze again overnight, and I spent too long in the hide, risking frostbite for views of otters on the ice that never materialised. The Causeway bridge area was the only open water on the reserve apart from the ditches. The ice disappeared as fast as it had formed as temperatures rose over the next few days, though heavy rain falling on top of the ice made the paths treacherous for a while.

On Christmas Eve I had the most enchanting views of the four cubs catching fish and bringing them out onto the bank to the right of Lower hide. The episode lasted for nearly an hour, and at times they came so close that I scarcely dared to breathe, for fear of startling them. It was easy to see that one of them was smaller than the rest, which were near full-grown now, and the smaller one stayed apart from the others for most of the time.

I saw no otters on Christmas Day, perhaps not surprisingly since high winds and water levels had turned Causeway pool into a miniature simulation of the North Sea, though I did feel at the time that they might have made more of an effort ...

They all turned up on Boxing Day, however, and continued to show well into the New Year, with between three and five seen regularly.

Lower hide path was flooded at the beginning of January 2012, so I walked to the reserve through the fields and saw a splendid fox.

Just before the gate I heard the unmistakeable tonking call of ravens, and had magnificent views of seven displaying right over my head, twisting in the air to fly upside down, as they showed off to each other.

I continued on to Causeway hide and saw all five otters. Visitors in the hide thought there were only three at first, but because the cubs were diving so well and staying submerged for longer it was now hard to see all five heads at once.

Falling water levels made the path to Lower accessible by the following week, and as I arrived three otters porpoised swiftly into the left-hand bay, flushing a bittern as they went.

I thought maybe that was it for the morning, but how wrong I was. Moments later I could hear quite a tussle in the reeds close to the hide, so the otters had obviously left the water. I could not quite make out what was happening until they all burst out into the open. One held an enormous eel in its mouth but was struggling to make any headway with it, as there was another otter clinging on to the opposite end!

The pair with the eel scrambled along the bank, squealing, more like piglets than otters, with the eel firmly grasped at both ends, while the third otter returned to the water and looked on. A tug of war then ensued with the unfortunate eel looking more like a taut piece of rope than a fish. There was not going to be any sharing of this catch.

One of the two then lost its grip and tried desperately to grab hold again, but as the victor jumped around with its reward, the loser gave up and joined its sibling in the water. The otter then dragged the eel even closer to the hide to eat it, which I was able to watch at close quarters in grisly detail!

I noted on many occasions that young otters show well when they are learning to fish, because their inexperience means that they may take some time to catch what they need. On this morning they hunted in front of the hide for over two hours, providing some excellent prolonged views.

Cold weather arrived, and by the third week in January a thin layer of ice lay over most of the water on the reserve. I saw the whole family breaking through it as they forged along, moving at a very impressive speed for the conditions, and leaving a trail of destruction through the pristine surface as they went.

Temperatures fell still further, and the reserve froze hard at the start of February. Four otters crossed the ice along the back edge, in single file, walking along nose to tail. The only open water on the reserve was a small pool opposite the Causeway hide, which was kept open by the resident mute swans. There was a slight snowfall, and I found otter prints on Lower hide path.

There were also multiple prints across the ice to the west of Causeway bridge and all around the bridge area, together with fresh spraint. Once again I also found anal jelly, which I had seen in very cold conditions in previous years.

Temperatures remained low throughout most of February, but it became milder and wetter towards the end of the month. I visited Lower hide on one particular morning which would turn out to be yet another milestone.

The birds on the water seemed very skittish, and I felt certain that there were otters about. Sure enough two appeared on the Border, and it wasn't long before I saw three more to the right of the posts. All five then joined up, and over the next half hour they dived and fished in the middle of the pool before they all melted into Island Mere. This was to be my last ever sighting of the five of them together. I had been watching them as a family unit since the beginning of the previous August, seven months earlier, and though I continued to see them fishing apart from each other I would never again see them all in a single group.

I continued to watch from Lower hide, and often saw two or three otters in their now familiar haunts. March arrived, and at long last it began to feel as though spring was just around the corner, which was such a welcome relief after the long hard winter.

One bright and windy day I walked to the causeway. As I reached the bridge two mallards took to the air as an otter surfaced right in front of me. This was the first time I had ever disturbed an otter here, although I knew there had been many near misses when I had found fresh spraint and wet trails from the water.

Throughout the spring of 2012 it was otters galore, at almost every visit. These were usually of distant single animals, but on one occasion I was in Lower hide by myself, watching an otter fishing on the back edge, when another turned up and a serious fight began.

They were boxing and biting each other, then a chase towards the hide followed, and they leapt out of the water like dolphins, one in front, the other in pursuit. The escapee was caught just left of the hide and another battle took place before the flight started again.

The speed of their swimming, and their leaps from the water, reminded me of the recent Olympic men's butterfly event, though I think the otters would easily have won the gold medal! This continued all the way to Causeway hide. I went there to find out what happened next, and saw one otter returning to Lower pool, after the other had retreated into the reeds.

This conflict had been in earnest, rather than play fighting, perhaps because the cubs were fully grown now, and beginning to seriously contest their territories, or maybe I had witnessed the eviction of an incomer from another group territory?

A wet summer led to high water levels on the reserve, and from June onwards the sluice gates were kept fully open in an attempt to return levels to normal for the benefit of bitterns. Otters seemed quite happy with these conditions though, and were often seen.

One October evening I visited the reserve after a very heavy shower, and as the sun came out I was treated to the manifestation of an intense double rainbow. I was in Causeway hide and the spectacle was made all the more unusual because the rainbow appeared to end not far behind the stony island some thirty metres away.

As I was pondering this unlikely vision I heard the distinctive call of a kingfisher, which flew in from the left and landed on the post in front of the hide. The sight of the bird with the rainbow as a backdrop was awe inspiring enough, but I could hardly believe my eyes when a second kingfisher flew onto the scene, and was immediately chased by the first bird. They flew round and round in front of the hide, passing the rainbow each time, and sometimes giving the illusion of actually having flown through it; a memorable and most surreal experience.

Chapter Five

Over the next ten months I continued to see adult otters, swimming and fishing mostly alone, but there were no reports of any new cubs. Since 2007 the breeding cycle of otters at Leighton had been approximately biennial, and as it was just over two years since the last four cubs, I was constantly on the alert for any signs of a new litter.

Long summer evenings meant not only was there plenty of opportunity to look for otters, but also time to enjoy the hirundines which come from near and far to feed on the myriad of insects that inhabit the reedbed. The most spectacular of these, of course, are the dragonflies, and these in turn sometimes attract the attention of that swift-like predator, the hobby. I was once lucky enough to watch one for over an hour, as it caught one dragonfly after another, effortlessly seizing them in its talons and eating them on the wing.

September saw the return of the contractors' heavy plant machinery, as the RSPB continued their excavations to remove the silt and deepen the channels to the east of the causeway. Access to the reserve was gained by dismantling the dry stone wall bordering the road behind Island Mere, at the site of the small lay-by. A wide channel was then cut through the reeds into Lower pool. A second channel crossed Lower hide path to provide access to the fields between the reserve and Grisedale farm, where the contractors initially parked their machinery.

At the end of September two otters boxed fervently, with much whickering, before swimming off in opposite directions. It seemed that one of the two was uncomfortable with the proximity of the other for some reason. Around the same time I also logged a single otter carrying fish into the reeds to the left of Big island on five separate occasions, and suspected that it wouldn't be long before cubs were seen again.

About a week later, on a damp morning as it was just coming light, a female otter swam very slowly, almost fully submerged, with two cubs right alongside her. They passed in front of Big island and into Island Mere Inlet.

The female came out moments later, and powered her way to the far side of the Causeway pool, where she caught a fish. She then came all the way back to where she had gone in with the cubs, which was a return trip of quite some distance. She swam sometimes in head up posture, with the large fish visible between her teeth, but every now and then she dived and stayed underwater for a little way.

Ostensibly this increased the efficiency of her swimming, since underwater she could propel herself more effectively, but the increased drag of the fish would then hinder her progress, causing her to surface again.

Towards the end of October the BBC film crews arrived, in preparation for the forthcoming series of Autumnwatch, which was going to be based in the barn at Grisedale farm. They were in the field opposite Lower hide early one morning, filming the misty sunrise, and I hoped they got the shot of me waving at them!

Unfortunately this was going to be their last day of even half decent weather, and by the time the programme was over they might as well have renamed it Stormwatch.

I saw the family of otters regularly whilst Autumnwatch was airing, and noted that one of the cubs seemed to swim more proficiently than the other. Visitor numbers soared that week and one morning we watched the two cubs exploring the cormorant posts, their mother looking on, as she circled around them. This continued for more than ten minutes, before all three headed off towards Causeway hide.

After the BBC had gone the lives of the otters returned to a normality somewhat removed from that which the producers and presenters had invented for them on screen.

I was in no hurry as I walked to Lower hide one day at the start of November, as cold winds from the north blew the remaining leaves from the trees, and menacing clouds weighed heavy overhead. In fact, I was beginning to wonder why I had ventured out at all, as the woods seemed to be devoid of any birdlife and it was difficult to hold my binoculars steady whilst holding on to my hat.

Then, just as I was crossing the first bridge, I heard a distant honking. I stopped in my tracks and listened again, then my spirits lifted and I quickened my step. The honking had developed into trumpet calls as I reached the door of the hide. Three whooper swans had landed in the right-hand pool, and looked as glad to be out of the wind as I was.

At the end of November the reserve froze again, and I watched the female otter and her two young making the most of the conditions. They were playing on the Spit, then running onto the ice and crashing through it, before climbing back out and repeating the performance, and it almost seemed as though they were doing it just for fun! I could now see that one of the cubs was somewhat larger than the other, and therefore most probably a male.

Good sightings of this family continued into December. The RSPB had lowered the water levels to provide better access for the contractors, and the otters were easy to see in the shallow water.

Digging out of Lower pool began around mid-December 2013, and continued well into the following year, and there was general concern about the effect this would have on the otters. A huge excavator was mounted on a floating platform, and the silt was initially loaded into a barge, from where it was pumped down a flexible pipe and spread over the fields at Grisedale farm.

These operations inevitably created a great deal of noise and disturbance, and were probably more protracted than was originally planned due to unforeseen mechanical breakdowns. By the time the project was over the fields had been completely covered with silt.

Otters seldom showed up in daylight, though I did still occasionally see the family when I visited before the contractors had started for the day.

By February, however, based on size alone, it was no longer possible to tell if I was watching two cubs, or the mother and the smaller cub, when only two of them were showing. Their behaviour was often more helpful in this respect, so when sharing of prey was seen this would indicate parental feeding, rather than sibling interactions.

The contractors finally left at the end of February, and peace again returned to the reserve, just in time for my favourite part of the year.

For me, spring begins in March, with the annual bittern migration, which I have watched and recorded for many years now. In autumn the bittern population at Leighton Moss is swelled by the arrival of migrant birds, which remain over winter. Over a few evenings in March, when conditions are suitable, they leave the reserve in near darkness. Most years this also coincides with the appearance on the causeway of large numbers of mating frogs and toads, and a torch is therefore needed to avoid stepping on them on the way home. One evening I found a male toad desperately clinging onto the back of a female frog, a union bound to end in disappointment.

In July 2014 there were reports of a female otter with two young cubs, but I didn't manage to see them myself until August. This was the first time I had seen a female with young in two consecutive years, so was there now another adult female sharing the group territory? This family seemed to spend most of its time in the Causeway pool just past the Border, and I wondered whether the removal of silt from this area had improved conditions for fishing.

I began to notice that on many occasions when I was watching this family I also saw a second otter fishing in the Lower and Causeway areas, and visitor accounts of a mother with two cubs began to increase significantly in both Lower and Causeway pools. The explanation for this became clear one evening, when I saw a female with two cubs on the Border at the same time as a second female with another two cubs in the pool to the right of Lower hide. The reserve was now supporting two families of otters, a very exciting development.

Over the next few weeks the two separate families ranged between both pools, but generally remained discrete. Then one morning they both mingled around Big island, with the cubs chasing each other and the females looking on. This was the only time I ever saw them come together, though there were many occasions when they fished quite close to each other. One day, whilst both families were in view, there was also a seventh otter, of unknown sex and origin, in the far distance. Seven otters at once, another record for me!

The two families were often seen in Lower and Causeway pools throughout 2014, and became a notable, and fairly dependable, attraction. Both females regularly hunted in the middle of the day, and it became almost unusual for visitors to spend a day at Leighton Moss without seeing at least one otter.

The two family units remained intact throughout the summer, but as the year drew in the cubs began to fish more independently away from their mothers. By the following spring most reports were of only single otters, and it was no longer possible to be certain if these were the females or their now well-grown cubs.

Two new families in one year, and immediately following the previous year's litter, indicated that Leighton Moss was now providing well for their needs, though whether this was a result of the excavation of the pools, or some other factor, was uncertain. What was certain, however, was that the disturbance hadn't driven them away, as had been feared.

This year was also memorable for quite another reason, since on 22nd September 2014 I made my highest egret count ever: 182 little egrets, a record which remains unbroken to this day.

The egret count usually peaks around this time of year, and the previous evening's count of just over 100 had seemed impressive enough at the time. On this evening, however, they just kept on coming, long after dusk had fallen, and their raucous calls punctuated the night air as they jostled for position in the roost. I confirmed the count the next morning, when helpfully they left the roost sporadically, in small groups.

On my way to the hide, through the fields, a badger snuffled along the hedgerow heading back towards the woods. This was both unusual and thrilling, because whilst badgers are not at all uncommon in the area, they are almost never seen out in the open.

The following year, at the end of July 2015, a female with two cubs crossed the back edge at Lower, so otters at Leighton Moss had once again bred in consecutive years. This was excellent news in itself, but was made all the more exciting for me because it confirmed a prediction I already had of their coming.

Two months earlier, on 28th May, entirely by chance I had found tracks of a single adult otter on a wooded hillside some 300 metres from the water at Leighton Moss, in an area of blackthorn scrub.

Eurasian otters use natal holts in which they give birth, and where they remain with their cubs for the first two months of their life, often only leaving the holt to make a single fishing trip each day. Natal holts are seldom close to the otters' fishing areas, in order to guard against cannibalism by male otters, and can be located up to a kilometre or more from the water.

They are notoriously difficult to find because they show no spraints, and have a concealed entrance with no obvious track leading to it, and once the cubs have left the natal holt the female will not return there until once again ready to give birth.

I have never located a natal holt at Leighton, but the area where I found the otter tracks was ideal habitat where one could be concealed, and the presence of the tracks in that area did not fit any alternative explanation. I therefore considered it most likely that these cubs were probably born in a natal holt somewhere on that hillside. I did not, however, make any attempt to find it, as this would have been neither ethical nor necessary. The existence of the cubs proved the existence of a natal holt, and its precise location was irrelevant.

Further observations of this family revealed that there were actually three cubs; two that were often seen in close combat, and a third, slightly smaller animal, which spent more time with the female. This was reminiscent of the behaviour previously demonstrated by the female and four cubs of 2011.

On several occasions I witnessed an unidentified otter swimming close to this family, but the mother always chased it away. One day the three cubs were on Big island and the female was fishing alone to the right, when an intruding otter went onto the island.

The female immediately raced after it, and I could hear quite a squealing commotion, before a single otter emerged and made off rapidly. I waited for some time, but no others appeared. I returned that same evening, however, and saw the female and three cubs again, so could confirm that they were none the worse for their experience.

My concern for their welfare was well founded, as conflicts between otters can have fatal consequences. A number of studies have shown that attacks from other otters may be the second commonest cause of violent deaths, after road traffic accidents. Such attacks become increasingly common as otter population densities increase, which is why I was particularly relieved at the outcome of this confrontation.

I continued to watch this family over the following months, and the two dog otter cubs would often be seen fighting each other, though not yet quite in earnest. Visitors would often be shocked to see such behaviour, which contrasted somewhat with their expectations, since the ferocity of the cubs certainly seemed real enough to inexperienced observers.

The mother continued to catch prey for herself and the female cub, without the need to deal with competition from the males, which were by now becoming capable of providing for themselves.

As summer drew to a close, the population of the reserve was swelled by the arrival of winter migrants.

One of the first heralds of their arrival was the falsetto calls of pink-footed geese, as they flew high over my house in huge skeins, heading south. Visits to the wader pools can be rewarding at this time, as birds return from their breeding grounds, and I have had many escapades here over the years.

At Lower hide the commonest wader seen in winter is usually the snipe, which is often present in significant numbers, but can be surprisingly difficult to find. The best indication of their presence is sometimes their distinctive flight call, sounding like a boot being pulled from squelchy mud.

The reserve also harbours their diminutive relative, the jack snipe, and RSPB wardens would often recount their experiences of flushing these birds from the reedbed. For me, however, they were an elusive and almost mythical species, and despite more than twenty years of carefully sifting through snipe with my scope, I had yet to see one.

Then, one late winter afternoon, I sat in Lower hide as visitors clicked their cameras at a group of snipe close outside the window. Looking over the visitors' shoulders I fancied that one of the birds appeared slightly different, but before I could focus my binoculars it took two steps into the reedbed and vanished.

The remaining snipe continued to probe the mud with their extraordinary bills, but the missing bird did not rejoin them, despite continuing my vigil until eventually the failing light forced me to give up.

By morning I had convinced myself that my first jack snipe was waiting for me in the reeds at Lower, and I wasted no time making my way there, walking through a heavy rainstorm.

I concentrated intently on the spot where I thought it had entered the reedbed the previous evening. After about an hour I was beginning to reason that the chances of it still being in the same spot, if it had ever been there in the first place, were so astronomically low that I was doomed to failure yet again.

And then it appeared.

This was far from the brief glimpse promised by the textbooks and websites. It stepped out from a patch of sedge and stood in front of me in full view, no more than three metres away. It bobbed in slow motion as I took in the details of the bird I had yearned to see for so long.

The golden stripes down its back and along its head appeared freshly painted, and the diagnostic dark crown stripe danced up and down in my binoculars. I was able to take in every detail at my leisure before it walked back into the sedge and I was able to breathe again.

Some things are worth waiting for.

The following year, in August 2016, an otter began to take its catch into an area of reeds to the left of the stone island at the Causeway hide, on a daily basis. This behaviour almost always preceded the appearance of a new family, so I made sure that I was there early each morning. Predictably, at the end of the month at first light, a female otter with three small young emerged from the same spot and swam towards Lower hide.

Sightings of cubs in their first few weeks after leaving the natal holt are always special, not least because such views are so rare. As cubs begin to learn to fish for themselves they are quite often seen in the water with their mother, but when they are very young she prefers to leave them hidden in the reedbed while she finds food for them, and they are seldom seen. My very next observation provided a rather dramatic demonstration of this particular female's preference for foraging alone.

The female was fishing at the back of Lower pool with a single cub following. Twice, she took her catch into the reeds and each time there was a cub closely in attendance. After her third visit she headed for Lower hide, but then two cubs started to chase after her. One made it only as far as Big Island before giving up, but the second continued to pursue its mother, and began calling loudly as it went.

The female was quite close to the hide when the young otter finally made contact with her, but she was none too pleased to be interrupted. She turned angrily on the cub and attacked it vigorously, holding it under the water as the two writhed and whirled around in turmoil. All the while the cub produced the most haunting of squeals, as though it was being murdered, which is exactly what looked to be the case. They disappeared into the left-hand bay, out of sight, and the chilling calls continued. Then all went quiet, and I feared the worst.

I knew the mother would eventually have to return to the other two cubs, so I waited until at long last I glimpsed her ripples moving back towards me. She surfaced alone at first, and my heart sank, but then I breathed a huge sigh of relief when I saw the cub was still following behind.

The female coursed powerfully back across the pool whilst the cub struggled to catch up. On reaching the far edge she resumed fishing, but could still not shake off the youngster, which had obviously not been deterred by its experience.

I was very happy to see the whole family again at Lower in the morning. The female was very active trying to catch breakfast whilst the three young otters chased after her.

I wasn't able to visit the reserve for the next three weeks, but on my return, at the end of September, I found that the water levels had dropped considerably and that both Lower and Causeway pools were covered by algal blooms. These are usually the result of increased levels of nutrients in the water, as can be caused by agricultural run-off from surrounding fields. Severe blooms can deplete oxygen levels sufficiently to kill fish, and sometimes involve growth of toxic species, which can be harmful both to wildlife and to humans. Such consequences have not yet been a problem at Leighton Moss to the best of my knowledge, but there had been hardly any reports of otters, diving ducks or cormorants whilst I was away, and I wondered whether the presence of the blooms deterred them from fishing.

I went to Lower and managed to see two otters diving in the deeper part of the pool where there was still no algal growth. One eventually caught a sizeable fish and took it into the reeds on the left-hand side of the Border, with the second in hot pursuit. The wakes were spectacular as the water levels were so low. Based on their behaviour I concluded that they were probably mother and cub. I thought that she might be taking the fish back to her other two cubs, and hoped that they would all show up. Shortly afterwards, however, just two otters spilled out of the reeds at the same point. They looked similar in size and spent some time together swirling around in the water, causing waves all over Lower pool, and I was sure that these were two of the cubs.

A couple of weeks later very heavy rain and hail produced a most atmospheric morning. The wind swept across the water in the dawn light, and sheets of rain pulled heavy curtains across Causeway pool.

An otter fished around a small island of cut reeds not far from the hide, and quickly caught an enormous eel, which was taken over to the reeds by the willows to the left of the pool. After a short while three otters swam out, a female with two cubs porpoising behind. She led them back to the island of cut reeds and they all climbed out. I put down my binoculars and gazed at the unfolding intimate scene as the young otters snuggled up to their mother, rubbing their heads against her body, before they all slipped back into the water.

It was over six weeks since I had last seen the female otter with all three of her cubs, and she now appeared to have only two. This inevitably suggested that something tragic must have befallen one of them, since they were far too young for independence, and this was the first time I had ever known this to happen.

In mid-October the little egret roost swelled to 175 individuals, seven fewer than my record of September 2014, but memorable for another reason as, for one night only, they were joined by no fewer than ten great white egrets.

A marsh harrier flushed them from the roost and they circled in an unfeasibly white cloud, the lethargic wingbeats of the larger birds contrasting markedly with those of their smaller relatives. Eventually they returned to the treetops, which they all but filled, before they dropped, one by one, into the undergrowth. Yet another of those probably never to be seen again moments.

At the start of November temperatures fell, and Lower pool froze around the edges. The female otter walked out of the reeds and onto the ice, accompanied by her cubs. The female went first, and fell through the surface, whereupon the cubs crept back to the reeds and stood watching their mother. The female hauled herself back out and returned briefly to the reluctant cubs, perhaps to encourage them, before going back to the water.

The cubs stood and peered over the ice, which they had probably never come across before, as if to see how far it was to the deeper part of the pool. One then made its way gingerly across to join its mother, but the other showed no interest in following, and retreated back into the reeds.

The reserve continued to freeze for weeks, and I wondered whether the young otters were becoming more accustomed to the conditions by now. One cold murky morning in December I opened the window at Causeway hide when it was just light enough to see a moorhen fleeing from me across the ice.

In the reeds to the left of the window I saw what I thought at first was a female mallard with its head under its wing, and thought it strange that it had not moved when I opened the window. On closer inspection I realised to my delight that it was in fact an otter cub, curled up asleep only two metres from the hide!

On the shores of freshwater lakes otters prefer to rest or sleep on 'couches' in the reeds, or in thick vegetation, rather than in underground holts or dens, even in the coldest and most inclement of weathers, but I could hardly believe my luck that this otter had chosen to sleep here, of all places!

I could hear cracking ice in the distance, alerting me to another two otters moving down the edge of the reeds towards Lower pool. Their progress was hampered by the thin ice, which constantly gave way beneath them as they tried to make their way over its surface. Meanwhile, the otter in front of me had woken up, and after glancing briefly towards the hide, it yawned and stretched then nestled down again. Moments later it stood up and walked even closer to me before entering the water through a patch of broken ice. Over the next hour it fished and brought small prey out onto the surface. There was a breathing hole by a post, and often it would pop up and take a breath, which I could hear quite clearly, before it dived again and again. In the distance I could still see the other two otters fishing in the more open water at the Border, which was where I had to leave them, as they were much better equipped to deal with the cold than I was!

The fact that otters need to survive immersion in cold water presents a significant challenge, since water draws heat from their bodies more than 25 times faster than air of the same temperature. Otter fur has evolved to cope with this by trapping an insulating layer of air next to their skin, thus eliminating direct contact with the water itself. The air is held in short, fine underfur, which has a density of around 50,000 hairs per square centimetre of skin in the Eurasian otter. The water is kept away from otters' underfur by an outer layer of longer, waterproof guard hairs, which must be kept clean and well groomed if they are to fulfil this function.

Otters in the UK all belong to the same species, but some live in fresh water whilst others spend some, or most, of their time in saltwater. The waterproofing quality of otters' outer fur is reduced when contaminated by salt, so otters that swim in the sea must have access to sources of fresh water where they can regularly wash their fur. I have tracked otters for long distances down Scottish beaches, to find that they often visit freshwater pools near the shore for this purpose, and these same places must doubtless have been used by generations of otters over thousands of years and more.

It was now more than ten years since that fateful day when I saw my first otter at Lower, and what an eventful time it had been. When I embarked on my otter quest sightings were infrequent, and usually at either dusk or dawn, often in very low light conditions. Nowadays, otters can be seen at Leighton Moss relatively easily, at almost any time of day.

Otters have also been recorded at many other wetland sites around the area, and staff from the RSPB have obtained evidence of them in woods some distance from the reserve, using a camera trap.

In the early days I was very often alerted to the presence of otters by the behaviour of the other inhabitants of the reserve; birds on the water would flee in panic, whilst black-headed gulls, formerly much more numerous on the Lower pool than they are nowadays, would hover over otters in a very characteristic fashion. The sudden appearance of otters can still cause panic to this day, but many of the denizens of the reedbed have become accustomed to them over the years, and will now often remain in the vicinity as otters swim past, though they do still tend to keep a wary eye on them, which can sometimes assist in their location.

The fact that birds feature in the diet of otters has been reported by numerous sources, but this doesn't seem to be a common occurrence at Leighton Moss in my own experience. I have seen tawny owls and kestrels take starlings and marsh harriers harass bitterns. I have seen bitterns spear rats, and snap dragonflies from out of the air, but in all of my time on the reserve I have never seen an otter take a bird, or even attempt to do so. I have on two occasions, both in freezing conditions, found remains of feathers in otter spraint, so don't deny that it happens, but taken in the context of the huge number of spraints (and birds) I saw over the years this is hardly significant.

I do, however, have personal experience of two occasions when otters were wrongly accused.

One morning I watched a marsh harrier harassing a coot. Over a period of more than half an hour it repeatedly swooped down on the bird, and the coot dived again and again in order to escape. The sustained onslaught eventually drowned the coot, and its lifeless body floated on the water. The marsh harrier then made multiple unsuccessful attempts to claim its kill, but eventually gave up and flew away.

I had once before witnessed a similar attack when the marsh harrier had ended up in the water, and it had experienced great difficulty in becoming airborne again. I knew, therefore, that this raptor was uncomfortable with immersion and so it was no surprise that on this occasion the marsh harrier abandoned its prey rather than risk drowning itself.

I left the hide, but returned again later the same morning to find the hide full of visitors who were excitedly watching two otters playing with the body of the coot. The otters took turns to pick it up in their mouths, and I was reliably informed that the visitors had seen the otters kill the coot, an opinion which was never going to be altered by an inconvenient fact.

The second event concerned the mysterious and progressive disappearance of a whole clutch of mute swan cygnets, and as their numbers dwindled popular rumour laid their demise firmly at the door of the otters. However, at that time a pair of great black-backed gulls were raising their chicks at Lower. I watched them taking the young swans one after another, picking them off the water and swallowing them whole for later regurgitation, a grisly and most impressive feat, but not an otter in sight.

My ability to watch otters at Leighton Moss was greatly assisted by the fact that they are active in daylight here, whereas at many other locations they are mostly nocturnal and so are seldom seen. Hans Kruuk believes that this is due to the continued availability of eels as prey species at Leighton Moss, and considers these to be a great support for the otter population. Otters prefer to hunt for prey when it is inactive, and eels are very nocturnal, and therefore much easier to catch in the daytime. At marine sites, such as Shetland, Skye and Mull, the most important prey species are nocturnal rocklings, butterfish and eelpouts, so otters are diurnal there too. Where important prey species are active in the daytime, in contrast, then otters will hunt them at night instead, when they are at their most lethargic.

At Leighton Moss I often saw otters taking eels and large pike. They undoubtedly took other species too, otters are opportunistic feeders and will catch whatever is available, but these two featured regularly enough to be noteworthy. The availability of so many large pike over the years is a testament to the good health of the fish population on the reserve, since these predatory fish are at the top of the food chain. The availability of eels, indicated not just by what I saw, but also by the very fact that otters here are diurnal, poses something of a conundrum. It is a well-published fact that eel populations have crashed across Europe, with declines of up to 95% in the last 25 years, according to the Environment Agency, yet the otters at Leighton Moss are still managing to catch specimens of significant size.

My most unexpected discovery was undoubtedly the litter of four cubs in 2011, a truly wondrous event to which I have unapologetically devoted a good deal of this account. Five otters don't break any records, but their appearance was unusual by any standards and they provided some of my most enlightening experiences.

The fact that this litter was unusually large also allowed me to be absolutely certain that I was watching the same family day after day, and that they were the only family on site at that time. From 2007 to 2013 the otter breeding cycle at Leighton was biennial, but from 2013 to 2016 new cubs appeared every year, and in 2014 I saw two families in proximity to each other for the first time.

This increase in breeding rate probably resulted from a growth in the number of occupied female core territories within the group territory at Leighton Moss. Mainland otters can breed at any time of year, and are not considered to have a breeding season as such.

However, over ten years I recorded eight litters of cubs, and each of them first appeared between July and October, so possibly breeding at Leighton is more seasonal than might usually be expected.

Watching otters can easily give the impression that they have an easy life, as they fish and play with apparent gay abandon. Appearances can be deceptive, however, and nothing could be further from the truth. Otters require huge amounts of energy to maintain their body temperature in cold water, and they need to catch their prey quickly and efficiently if it is to give them more energy than the chase costs. Although they will pursue fish if necessary, which I have seen on many occasions, they prefer to hunt by stealth, in short shallow dives. They live on a knife edge as regards energy balance, and have a remarkably low life expectancy for such a large animal. Kruuk records that most otters survive for an average of only four years, and manage to hold core territories for an average of only two, and whilst some do die violently, for example on the roads, many simply quietly starve to death when their energy balance tips in the wrong direction.

I therefore found it encouraging that, of the eight litters of otters that I watched at Leighton Moss, I know for certain that the first seven survived to the point of separation without losing any members. The eighth litter lost only a single cub, and this clearly indicates that the habitat at Leighton Moss is very conducive to their survival. What happened to the young from any of the litters after dispersal is unknown, but as long as each of the families remained together at Leighton Moss then their survival rate was remarkable.

In close competition with the five-otter family, and, of course, not entirely unrelated, was the phenomenon of Kinky. The ability to individualise him proved very helpful, particularly for the object lessons he provided in the hazards of sexing otters in the field at distance. The infrequency with which he showed up, over the mere fifteen months he was around, was consistent with the larger size of male territories and was entirely as expected.

Above all, over my ten years of observations, I learned that interpretation of what I was seeing necessitated careful consideration, tempered with a degree of caution. The unusual circumstances which enabled individualisation of particular animals greatly facilitated my understanding, and without these I would have had considerable difficulty. It is therefore fair to say that any explanations offered by occasional visitors to the reserve, however expert, necessarily involve a good deal of guesswork, and, in the words of Kruuk, should sometimes be treated with a dose of salt.

Resident populations of otters are augmented from time to time by the arrival of transients, which are juvenile otters from other areas searching for territories of their own. Some of the lone otters I saw during my observations, not all of which are included in this account, doubtless fell into this category. Kruuk's studies in Shetland were aided by the fact that individuals from this population possess uniquely patterned throat markings, so transients from outside his study area could easily be identified as such. Mainland otters do not have these markings, and without such aids it is never possible to be absolutely sure about exactly what is happening all of the time.

Wildlife documentaries often appear to provide full and precise accounts of what they portray, but this is sometimes an illusion as they must assemble the available footage and then adapt the story to fit it. My honest account, in comparison, may at times seem incomplete, but I hope it achieves what I set out to do, which was simply to share my joy of watching these magnificent animals in the wild at Leighton Moss.

Appendix

The Eurasian otter (*Lutra lutra*) has been resident in the British Isles since at least the end of the last ice age, some 10,000 years ago, and was common throughout the whole of the UK until the middle of the last century.

The 1950s heralded the widespread introduction of organochlorine insecticides, such as dieldrin and DDT, which were wholeheartedly embraced by the agricultural industry, and used in everything from seed dressings to sheep dips. These chemicals were remarkably effective against the pests they targeted, and were generally regarded as saviours of modern agriculture.

Unfortunately, however, they proved to be toxic to a wide range of animals, but most especially the apex predators, due to the chemicals' ability to accumulate in the food chain. From the mid 1950s to the late 1970s otter populations crashed, not just in the British Isles but also across much of Europe. This led to otters being afforded legally protected status in 1978, as prior to this they had been hunted with dogs in areas where they were considered to threaten game fish.

Between 1977 and 2010 the Environment Agency carried out five national otter surveys to determine the extent of the decline, and their findings provided serious cause for concern. The first survey, carried out between 1977 and 1979, found signs of otters, in the form of spraint or prints, at only 6% of UK sites, and only 2.8% of those in the north west of England, even though these were all sites which were known to have been occupied previously. The only remaining healthy populations were in remote parts of Scotland, though small numbers were still found in Wales and in parts of north and southwest England, where agricultural intensity was lower.

In the early 1980s the fate of the otter was considered so precarious that the Nature Conservancy Council instigated a programme of captive breeding, and animals were released to the wild, mostly in East Anglia, but also elsewhere.

The Table opposite shows the findings of each of the Environment Agency surveys relevant to Leighton Moss and the surrounding areas.

The results show that otters were found at both Leighton Moss RSPB and nearby Haweswater in the first survey of 1979, and that these were the only local sites that fell within the nationwide 6% of positive results in that survey. Leighton Moss was therefore one of very few sites to retain otters at a time when they had all but disappeared from much of the rest of the country.

However, it is important to appreciate that whilst positive results can be accepted as accurate records, the nature of the surveys meant that false negatives were possible. For example, the negative result from Leighton Moss stream in 2009 is obviously false, as it postdates the return of otters by some 3 years.

Year of Survey	79	86	93	00	09
Brackenthwaite, Leighton Beck	N	N	P	P	N
Leighton Moss RSPB Reserve	P	P	P	N	P
Estuary, Leighton Moss Stream	N	P	P	N	N
Haweswater	P	P	P	N	P
Estuary, River Keer	N	N	N	N	N
Arnside, Leighton Beck	N	N	N	N	N
Carnforth, Lancaster Canal	N	N	N	N	N
Hest Bank, Coast	N	N	N	N	N
Skerton, Lancaster Canal	N	N	N	N	N
Halton, River Lune	N	P	P	P	P
Heysham, Coast	O	O	N	N	N
Oxcliffe, River Lune Estuary	N	N	N	N	P
Haverthwaite, River Leven	N	N	P	P	N

N = No evidence of otters

P = Otters recorded as present

O = Not surveyed

https://data.gov.uk/dataset/otter-surveys-1977-2010

Brackenthwaite, like Haweswater, is a close neighbour of Leighton Moss, and the fact that each of the five surveys found signs of otters at one or other of these three sites suggests a degree of persistence of otters in the local area, including also the Rivers Lune and Leven.

At Leighton Moss RSPB, the Environment Agency surveys suggest that otters disappeared from the site some time between 1993 and 2000, but cannot narrow this period any further.

Fortunately, however, John Wilson kept records of otter sightings on the reserve between 1977 and 1998, which provide additional helpful data for this site.

The data are in the form of random yearly sightings from the reserve, and counts are influenced both by the presence or absence of young and by the frequency of recording, so cannot be used to indicate the numbers of individuals present at any particular point. Nevertheless, the data unequivocally illustrate the sudden and dramatic decline of the Leighton Moss otter population, and are shown in the Table on the facing page.

Otter sightings were not collected separately prior to 1977, but earlier annual reports for the reserve provided no cause for concern. Litters of otters were recorded on site in 12 of the 19 years from 1977 to 1995, which appears indicative of a healthy population, almost to the point of their sudden demise.

Year	Sightings	Year	Sightings	Year	Sightings
1977	187	1985	192	1993	217
1978	99	1986	121	1994	176
1979	72	1987	106	1995	58
1980	108	1988	158	1996	2
1981	188	1989	296	1997	1
1982	255	1990	349	1998	0
1983	125	1991	154		
1984	131	1992	273		

(John Wilson, pers.comm.)

However, three animals were recorded as suffering from blindness, the last being a dog otter in 1995. This is significant since it is a specific sign of poisoning by organochlorine pesticides, such as dieldrin.

Accumulation of these chemicals in the bodies of otters causes reproductive abnormalities and also interferes with metabolism of Vitamin A, causing retinal dysplasia, which ultimately leads to blindness. In southern England some 30% of otters examined between 1996 and 1999 exhibited this condition to some extent, and all were found on analysis to harbour significantly elevated levels of dieldrin.

Dieldrin was gradually withdrawn from the market from 1962, and was banned completely by 1989, but this chemical is so persistent that it may take up to 25 years for 95% of it to degrade in the environment.

The Environment Agency's third otter survey, of 1991–94, found evidence of otters at 23% of UK sites, and in the north west of England the figure was almost 30%. This was considered to provide good evidence of natural recovery of otters, and the captive breeding programme was therefore abandoned. By the time of the fourth survey, in 2000–02, the percentage of UK sites positive for otters was 36%, and 34% in the north west of England.

It would thus appear that Leighton Moss continued to support ostensibly healthy populations of otters up to around 1994/5, and was unaffected by the nationwide decline which took place elsewhere between the 1950s and the 1970s. The population then disappeared around the same time that otter populations elsewhere were beginning to show signs of recovery, although the reason for this lag is unclear.

John Wilson reports that two otters were killed on the roads and two on the railway during the course of his study, whilst a further two were drowned in illegal fyke nets, and this may have contributed to the eventual demise of the population. He also considers that commercial fishing for eels in the tidal channel between the reserve and the wader pools in the early 1990s may have been a further contributory factor.

Acknowledgements

Hans Kruuk is an Honorary Professor at the University of Aberdeen and Emeritus Fellow at the UK centre for Ecology and Hydrology. His career embraces the study of otters around the world, but most of his academic research was focused on the study of Eurasian otters in Shetland, on which he is the foremost authority. His book, *Otters: ecology, behaviour and conservation* (2006), published by Oxford University Press, distils over 650 academic papers on the subject into a single accessible publication. I am honoured that Professor Kruuk agreed to write the preface to this book, and much obliged for his kind comments expressed therein.

Andrew Mackay has been a freelance wildlife artist since 1988 and has illustrated many books, including the *RSPB Birds of Britain and Europe* series by Rob Hume (Dorling Kindersley). He regularly exhibits at the Rutland Water Birdfair and BTO Conference art exhibitions and several of his works have been accepted for the prestigious National Exhibition of Wildlife Art. He is an active birder, and his familiarity with his subjects is made obvious by his outstanding observational skills and attention to detail. I am very grateful to Andrew for allowing me to include some of his works of art in this book, and more examples of his prodigious talent can be seen on his website (https://ajm-wildlife-art.co.uk/).

Ivan Frontani is originally from Rome, but moved to the UK in 1990 to study technical illustration. He has worked as a designer, illustrator and exhibition officer for Lancashire and Lancaster museums since 1996, as well as illustrating a number of publications. I was delighted with Ivan's ability to capture the spirit, character and movement of his subjects in a way which sets him apart from most of his contemporaries. He is an accomplished and versatile artist whose professionalism and ability to work to a tight brief made it a pleasure to work with him. His contribution to this book is invaluable and greatly appreciated.

I am indebted to John Wilson for allowing me to use his otter population data and for broadening my culinary horizons, and not least for building Lower hide in the first place. Thanks also to Robin Horner, Richard Miller, Jarrod Sneyd and everyone at Leighton Moss RSPB, and to Robert Ashworth, who managed to see the five otters in the end.

Image Credits

All colour paintings of wildlife are the original work of Andrew Mackay, as are the monochrome images of pied wagtail (p.12), black tern (p.30), lapwings (p.40) and kestrel (p.51). All other monochrome drawings are the original work of Ivan Frontani.

All maps, sketches and photographs are the work of the author, apart from the photograph of the excavator on p.83, which was donated by the RSPB. The images on pages 6, 22, 42 and 101 are of original embroideries created by the author.